D1529389

Rule Your Freakin' Retirement

Also by Michael Parness

Rule the Freakin' Markets
Power Trading/Power Living

Rule Your Freakin' Retirement

How to Retire Rich by Actively Managing Your Assets

Michael Parness

St. Martin's Press ✵ New York

RULE YOUR FREAKIN' RETIREMENT.
Copyright © 2009 by Michael Parness.
All rights reserved.
Printed in the United States of America.
For information, address St. Martin's Press,
175 Fifth Avenue, New York, N.Y. 10010.

www.stmartins.com

LIBRARY OF CONGRESS CATALOGING-IN-PUBLICATION DATA

Parness, Michael.
    Rule your freakin' retirement : how to retire rich by actively
managing your assets / Michael Parness.—1st ed.
                p.   cm.
    ISBN-13: 978-0-312-37575-1
    ISBN-10: 0-312-37575-1
    1. Retirement income—Planning.   2. Retirement—Planning.   3. Old
age pensions.   4. Investments.   5. Finance, Personal.   I. Title.
    HG179.P237 2009
    332.024'014—dc22   2008035448

First Edition: March 2009

10 9 8 7 6 5 4 3 2 1

This book is dedicated to my mother, Carol, who passed away during the final edits. She is sorely missed.

To my daughters, and lights of my life, Joelle Rebecca and Emma Grace.

And, to the 100,000s of newbies who I've had the pleasure of working with at trendfund.com and Trend Trading to Win, all of us searching for ways to a better life in this crazy world. Peace and prosperity to all.

Contents

Acknowledgments

I want to thank the following people who were invaluable in the creation of *Rule Your Freakin' Retirement*. Without them, there is simply no way you would be reading this now!

My agents, Frank R. Scatoni and Greg Dinkin at Venture Literary, who said, "Hey, we can sell that book!" and then made it happen!

St. Martin's Press, who believed in me enough to give me another shot at Rulin' something after the smashing success of *Rule the Freakin' Markets* worldwide!

My editor at St. Martin's Press, Phil Revzin, who has been ridiculously patient and supportive, and patient, and did I say patient? The dude has been a real trooper, and it's been an honor working with him.

Jay Greenleaf, who without his research, his clarity, and his insights the book would be a hollow shell of what it is. He has been a friend and just a super resource.

Michael "Tiny" Saul, who has worked with me for nine years at trendfund.com and who has helped us build one of the most influential and successful trading rooms the world has ever known. He's also been an invaluable friend.

Doug Koval, who has been a friend and confidant since high school and who has helped when I needed the time to continue writing this beast of a book.

My staff at trendfund.com: Sally Reppert, Ilene Hamilton, Scott, Debbie Lemel-Gross, Desiree Rowland, Scott Littlefield, et al., many of whom have been here since Day One of my journey in the markets and who have helped me in my own ability to retire. Carol

Guererro, who has taken such unreal care of my girls, she is an invaluable part of the family.

My daughters, Joelle Rebecca and Emma Grace, who are the absolute light of my life, without whom I would not know how rewarding life really is. They are magnificent and majestic and my babies.

My partners Elana Pianko and Stan Erdreich at Full Glass Films (http://www.fullglassfilms.com) who have helped me grow as an artist, and as a producer, and most of all as a person through thick and definitely through the thin of the film industry.

I'd also like to thank my clients at trendfund.com and trendtrading towin.com who have done their own searching, as you will do yours. And, in that searching, they have helped me, as you are, by believing that there are other alternatives to making one's financial and real life better—outside the box.

I'd also like to thank the following people for their support, their love, and their graciousness. They are warriors all: Jane Goldberg, Ph.D, Dr. Julian Neil, Bill McCarthy, Bill Marley, Mark Perez, Bonnie Rabin, Esq., Dr. Richard Rosenthal, Dr. Lori Weintrob, Rory Parness, Merri Siegel, Jessica Bayer, Stephanie Perronne, Sharon Dastur, Zena Burns, Jeff Telvi, and Giulianna Telvi. My nieces and my nephew: Corinne, Ariella, Shayna, Olivia, Juliet, Maya, Charlotte, and Noah

And *you,* because if no one reads your book, it's not worth writing!

Preface

As a kid we'd go to Chinatown on a big night out. My parents never had much, if any, money, and living in Queens, New York, a big night on the town was anywhere in Manhattan. Inevitably we'd be told, myself and my sisters, Merri and Jessica, and my brother, Rory, that we could only order from one side of the menu. We couldn't order steak, shrimp, or lobster. We couldn't afford it.

I always appreciated my parents' effort, but it irked me and didn't seem right that other people could order those things and we couldn't. I remember clearly swearing to myself that one day I'd be able to order as much shrimp and lobster as I could stand to eat. I *loved* shellfish.

As a teenager I spent some time on the streets, homeless. I ran away from home, and after sleeping on my friends' floors didn't work, I slept on the subway and in Prospect Park in Brooklyn or wherever there was a park bench. At that point in my life I wasn't thinking too much about shellfish, I was thinking about survival. One of the things you learn when you are struggling in life, I think, is that you don't have time to think about what you don't have; you just try to get enough to survive.

I always thought I was invulnerable. I mean, when you have been through some rough times, you get a bit toughened up; you have no choice. I had seen a lot of things, many of which no growing kid should ever have to see. I had friends who died, and I saw people on the street just expire in front of me. I never thought about my own mortality until 2001 when I was struck by a rare bug—they still don't know where it came from—and I nearly died. I flatlined on a gurney. I saw the proverbial white light, or pieces of it anyway. I remember thinking, right before I passed out, "This can't possibly be all there is!" It seemed so not possible, and so it turned out. Hopefully, it'll stay not possible for me to die for quite a while. I kinda like my life, ya know?

It also felt very unfair to me that here I had overcome so much, gone from zero to hero as my clients like to say at trendfund.com, and I was gonna just expire? No friends, no family, nothing but a gurney and some doctor who had a very freaked-out expression on his face. This was it? No! No way! And then I blacked out and woke up I guess a couple of minutes later. I was alive, and grateful.

Right before this happened, my oldest daughter was born. Happiest day of my life, for sure. She was and still is the sun in my damaged heart. I tell her, and it's true, that she is literally in my heart. She is there no matter what, every day and every minute. My youngest daughter joined her when she was born. It's kinda amazing how life can change at a moment's notice.

What does this have to do with *Rule Your Freakin' Retirement*? Well, it's pretty simple, I think. Before my kids were born and I felt immortal, the thought of things like retirement, or insurance, or savings, never entered my mind. I was always a day-to-day kind of person, and I still am in many ways, but I've learned that some things are worth protecting, and my daughters are certainly at the very top of that list.

In order to protect them, I started to think about what I would like to secure for them when I am gone. I am sure they would be fine without any money from me, but fine and better than fine are two very distinct planets. When my parents pass away, which hopefully won't be anytime soon, I don't think I'll get much of anything. They don't have much. And, that's okay, I don't need it at this point anyway. I'm more concerned with their well-being than I am their demise. But I would like to think that my girls will have a better inheritance. So, I bought life insurance for the first time in 2001, if memory serves. It's kinda surreal planning for your own death. I remember those commercials (they still play them sometimes) where the father-husband is there and then some voiceover comes on and says something like, "What happens when you're gone?" and then the dude just fades away and doesn't exist anymore.

It's pretty morbid, I think, but having my girls makes it easier to suffer a little morbidity in order to protect their future.

And part of my own future, my retirement, is also part of their future. I figured if I could learn to *rule* my retirement, then I would stand a much better shot at being prepared for things like college for them, the traveling I want to do as I get older, and eventually, yes, my death.

In the meantime, the retirement piece stands out for me. I would rather feel secure as I get older and prepared to keep eating shellfish. I don't eat steak much, if at all, so I wouldn't miss that, but I sure would miss my shrimp and lobster!

This book is about making a plan that allows you to take control of your retirement and the years leading up to it. It's better to start *today,* no matter your age, than wait until you have to rush and scurry around to try to make it work for yourself.

Trust me, I am not a planner. I am a person who does things on the so-called fly. I like spontaneity, I thrive on it, but I also know that as I get older I need to be just a wee bit more conservative in some of my spending habits. When I first made millions by trading stocks, I had no idea what it was to have money. I was buying things I didn't need just because it felt like I should. I was almost obligated to spend a lot of money since I had a lot of money. I don't feel that need any longer. I've been through many transformations in my life, and my latest seems to be—planning!

I can't speak for anyone else, but I feel a lot better with some cash in the bank, some savings, and without the fear that any day I could be homeless again! Trust me, I've asked other people who have spent time living on the streets, and most of us in the back of our heads still once in a while feel like we're going to be "struck homeless" at any minute, without warning, and be powerless to do anything about it!

One way to ensure that it won't ever happen, then, is to plan a clear and straight path to a retirement that frees you of worries about money on a day-to-day basis. Retirement should mean that you get to do just that—*retire!* If you're stressed about money, you're stressed, not retired!

Rule Your Freakin' Retirement is a book that takes you to places with your retirement that most retirement books would never deign to. It's got a lot of practical suggestions, but it also covers many of the aggressive (but I believe simple and safe) strategies that you should use to actively manage your retirement accounts.

In this day and age, being passive with your finances can, and very well may, lead you down a path to ruin, or to maybe worse, a path where you have to continue working for many years past the age most others are retired.

That's what *Rule Your Freakin' Retirement* is ultimately about: taking control of your finances to the point where it's part of your daily or weekly or monthly routine. That way it's not a burden. Taking control of a piece of your life that most people take for granted will allow you to rule not just your retirement, but your *entire life!*

That, my friends, is what we are striving for here. Don't take the lazy person's approach. Take the approach that it's *your* retirement, dudes and dudesses, and *no one* is gonna care more about your retirement then guess who? Go ahead: Guess!

You!

It's time for you to learn to
Rule Your Freakin' Retirement!
Get with the program!

Rule Your Freakin' Retirement

Don't Believe
Everything You Hear

In July 2002 *The Wall Street Journal* printed an amazing story. A reporter attended a seminar in Denver with a group that called itself Annuity University. If you don't know what an annuity is exactly, don't worry about it; there are a million types of annuities, and I'll be describing many of them later in the book. For now, just think of an annuity as an investment vehicle sold by an insurance company in which a buyer pays a specific amount up front in exchange for guaranteed periodic payments down the road, usually monthly or quarterly. As you'll learn, annuities are often poor investments. They give crappy rates of return and are loaded with fees. For some people—seniors in particular—they can be a *big* mistake.

So what did they teach at Annuity University? Insurance agents learned how to use scare tactics and charm to get seniors to buy their products. The writers of the article, Ellen E. Schultz and Jeff D. Opdyke, reported that agents were told to treat seniors like "blind twelve-year-olds." A portion of the article reads:

Trainees learn that the educational seminars can be used to generate fear among the attendees. "Toss hand grenades into the advice to disturb the seniors," Mr. Clark [the seminar leader] tells the trainees. He adds, "You're there to solve their problems, but you have to create

those problems first. No problem, no sale. So at the seminars, you're cre-
ating problems, and you tease them with the solutions" to encourage a
follow-up meeting with a salesman.

"They thrive on fear, anger and greed," Mr. Clark continues. "Show
them their finances are all screwed up so that they think, 'Oh, no, I've done
it all wrong.' This will make you money." The Annuity U. class learns that
whatever the retiree's particular concern—whether it's taxes, investment
returns or asset protection—the solution is almost always the same: an
annuity.

Another Annuity U. lecturer, Mel Brandon of Memphis, Tenn., tells
the class that educational seminars offer a good way to find out which
seniors are well off and worth concentrating sales pitches on. When
people arrive at his seminars, he says, he has "spotters" in the parking
lot "checking out what kind of car each person drives. That way we'll
know who has the money." The class chuckles.

Charming, eh?

The salesmen of annuities and the companies that market them
make a fortune by selling these things. A single sale can lead to thousands in commission for the salesperson. Insurance companies, some
of which are not especially trustworthy, often load annuities with in-
decipherable fee structures. Even a sophisticated investor may have a
hard time determining how much an annuity actually costs. The literature that gives fee details is intentionally opaque and confusing.
It's legalized loan sharking, and millions buy into it each and every
year without even learning what they are getting themselves into.
And blind faith equals a bad financial future.

These guys take advantage of vulnerable people so that they can
line their own pockets. It's despicable, really. And scary. But in the
world of retirement investing this sort of behavior is not at all uncom-
mon. People get taken all the time. Hundreds of times a day every day,
people across the country put money in investments that make little
sense for them. They're talked into spending their money in this way

by advisors who are more concerned about their own incomes than anything else. And not everyone who's taken is a vulnerable senior. A lot of smart, sophisticated people have their money in places they shouldn't.

Beware the Advisor

In the world of retirement planning, there's so much money in circulation that you have to expect hucksters like the ones described in the *Journal* article. Not all of them come out of shady operations like Annuity U. A lot of people who appear to be entirely credible are nearly as dangerous. If you need a quick example, just think back to the late nineties and the dot-com stock boom. The biggest, most-trusted investment houses showed that their interests and those of their investors were frequently at odds. The Merrill Lynch analyst Henry Blodget, who made a career out of hyping Internet stocks, told people within his company one thing (e.g., "I can't believe what a POS [piece of shit] that thing is.") while Merrill said something completely different to the public ("presents on attractive investment").

Blodget may be an extreme example, but it's a good idea to keep him in mind. You need to remember that Merrill, JPMorgan Chase, and the rest are companies—public companies—that are under constant pressure to show increasing profits. Every quarter they need to be taking in more and more money. And the advisors these companies employ to help you invest your hard-earned money often work on some sort of commission. You can be sure that the best commissions will not come from selling items with low customer fees, even if those are the best investments for *you!* Don't believe me? Go to your broker and tell him you're going to buy a bunch of bonds: You won't be trading or making any sort of adjustments; the money's just going to sit there, earning a predictable, steady, relatively low rate of return. See how happy your broker is then. At that point you may find out about additional fees that are applied to customers who don't make enough movements with their investments. Think about this for a second: You'll pay extra when you ask the brokerage to do nothing. Many brokers will suggest meaningless trades—known in the industry as "churn"—as a way of creating fees.

One last note about the dot-com boom and bust: About the only people happy about the bust from 2000 to 2003 were the traders like my clients at trendfund.com and short sellers.

Not all the overpriced advice on retirement is coming from the big Wall Street brokerages. In researching this book, I spoke to a friend who told me that a financial advisor oversaw his retirement accounts. He met the guy at work, as the advisor provided services for the company's 401(k). Through that position, the advisor would give seminars on retirement planning and offer his expertise outside of the work environment. This friend of mine, who had a substantial amount of money in an individual retirement account (IRA), liked the guy, and asked him to administer his account. There's nothing inherently wrong with this relationship, and I wasn't skeptical until I asked about the advisor's fee. The advisor, I was told, was being paid one percent of the amount that was being managed. I fired up a spreadsheet, did some quick calculations, and let my friend know that if he continued to pay one percent he'd pay over $200,000 in fees in the twenty years before he retired. Was this guy earning that sort of money? I took a look at his accounts and saw that he had a pretty basic setup of mutual funds.

It seemed to me that the advisor was putting in roughly ten hours per quarter on my friend's account—if that. And he really wasn't doing anything special to claim these extravagant fees. I suggested to my friend that he pay his advisor hourly for his work.

So be wary of the market and anyone who's trying to sell you anything, including individual expertise. It's a solid first step to moving toward the right investment strategies—and a healthy, financially secure retirement! It's a solid first step as you begin to Rule Your Freakin' Retirement!

Beware the General Wisdom

While I'm on the topic of Wall Street advisors, I want to address an important point, one that I'll return to periodically throughout this book. I bring it up here because it's something you're not going to hear from most financial advisors, especially those who are in the business of selling stocks and mutual funds. They're not going to tell you that the market is fundamentally a dangerous place. Yes, over the long term both the S&P 500 and the market as a whole have shown nice returns. But there's no guarantee that the historical rates of return will continue indefinitely.

Even if traditional rates continue for the foreseeable future, the general trend upward will be accompanied by some pretty sickening downswings. Think about the abrupt downturn that hit the market as a whole, and NASDAQ in particular, around 2000. People who invested at the height of the market lost a bundle in a hurry. Many 401(k)s became 201(k)s, or simply lost the 'k' and became S for "sucker." Seven years later, even those who were patient and kept their money in the market, were still showing a loss. In July 2007, the NASDAQ composite index had about half the value it did in July 2000, and that was after more than doubling between 2003 and 2007. Even the Dow, which saw record highs in 2007, has many stocks that are worth a fraction of their prices in 2000. And I'm not talking small-cap speculative stocks either, I'm talking about EMC Corporation, Cisco Systems, Intel Corporation, EXTRADE Financial Corporation, TD Ameritrade, and many, many others. And, that's not even throwing in the Enrons or WorldComs of the world. Blue chips can become *Soylent Green* chips (one of the best cult movies ever!) in very short order.

Some folks who were nearing retirement at the time of that crash had no way of recovering. They had to cut their losses and pull their money out of the market so they could be sure that they had some available for retirement. Most of these people, including many I know, got caught up in the hype of ballooning stock prices. They heard so many stories of people getting ridiculous returns that they felt they had to be a part of it. They came to think they'd be fools if they stayed out. They had come to believe that the market had only one direction—up. Then they got screwed.

What's the old adage? "If it seems too good to be true . . . it probably is!" I remember when I first called the *top* of the market in 2000. I went to my grocery store down the block from where I used to live in Tribeca and the grocer said he had just seen me on CNBC or Fox News and that he was opening a brokerage account because the market was *never going to go down!* I've made a very nice fortune with Trends, and one trend I know is that when everyone thinks the same thing, the opposite has to happen! Why? Think in terms of the oldest trend that everyone knows "Buy the rumor, sell the news!" When everyone has bought because something is going to happen (the rumor), when it actually does happen there's no one left to buy (the news). Badda-bing, badda-boom—ka-chingo! Millions of people and literally *trillions* of dollars went up in smoke in a very short time (as the final edit of this book is happening, the very same thing is unfolding in the market). And, I believe it's going to get a lot worse before it gets better. Buyer beware!

The folks who got killed were listening to the common wisdom, which can be a pretty dangerous thing. The myth of the ever rising stock market is only one part of the common wisdom. Some other elements you're likely to encounter: *Everyone should invest heavily in mutual funds. You shouldn't be investing in individual stocks. Whatever you do, avoid the daily ups and downs in the market by trading actively.* I don't believe that any of this is necessarily true, and as you work your way through this book, you'll see why. In fact, you'll see why I believe taking an *active* part in running your retirement account and finances is not only advisable, but necessary.

The other problem with sticking to the general consensus is that it's limiting. If you're only listening to groups that are echoing one another, you may miss out on ideas and techniques that are great for you—and profitable. You lose your ability to be thoughtful and creative. When I decided to commit myself to making a living by trading stocks, I did my research. I read everything I could, not about the market, but about human psychology, because that's who pushes the buttons—human beings. Then I went to study the market on my own, and I learned pretty quickly that there were ways of making money that other people hadn't discovered—or if they had made these discoveries, they weren't publicizing them. If my mind had been closed to new avenues, I'd never have made the money that I did.

In fact, I'd probably have gotten wiped out when the market went down, which many did. There are a *ton* of what I like to call bull-market geniuses. These are people who are *really* smart when the stock market goes straight up and when the economy is going good. Back in 1999–2000, and at many times in the history of the U.S. stock market, in good economic and market times, many people are *brilliant!* These same people can be struck dumb pretty fast when things turn a bit sour. I've seen many of my own clients get cocky when the market is going up, and they don't follow the rules to sell short when the market is tumbling. They get caught up in the hype and they lose. We had one client who I was told had turned roughly $60,000 into over $2 million using my methods, but then refused to sell short, or at least sit on cash when the market crashed. Last I knew she had lost it *all* back and was *down* to less than $25,000. I doubt she ever will get another chance. I like to say to clients at trendfund.com that one of the biggest things I can offer you is the chance to learn from *my* mistakes, so you don't have to make them yourself! The smart man learns from his own mistakes, the *wise* man learns from other's mistakes. I prefer to be wise when at all possible; it's a lot less costly, and could reap me the *big* ka-chingos!

In this book I'll tell you about some of the stuff I learned—the kind of things you're not going to read in any other retirement book. I'll talk about ETFs and gaps and how to use options to generate income for your retirement, while lowering the risk that a market downturn will kill your retirement. Plus, I'll give you some other options for making money by following market trends.

Before we get to that, you'll also need to learn about the basics— the parts of the conventional wisdom that are absolutely and unequivocally correct. You'll learn all you need to know about IRAs, 401(k)s, bonds, and those crappy annuities. You'll see savings calculators and worksheets, and you'll learn how to select a decent mutual fund. Once you've digested all this information, you'll have a good foundation, and you'll have a *plan* on how to guarantee the retirement you deserve.

Trust Yourself

When you look at the surveys and studies done about retirement planning in this country, it's pretty scary. Americans are notoriously bad at saving. We spend and run up debts and tend not to think about how these decisions will affect us years or even decades into the future. The statistics bear these notions out. According to an American Benefit Research Institute study from April 2007, most Americans don't have nearly enough in their savings. Nearly six in ten Americans (58 percent) have less than $50,000 in savings. About half of the workers over age 55 have less than $100,000 in savings. A full one-third of the country's workers have no savings at all: zip—zilch—Big fat zero!

You don't need a crystal ball to see that we're not living in an age where people should be taking their retirement savings this lightly. Pensions are going belly-up all the time. Social Security seems to be on shaky ground: Depending on who you talk to the system may be broke in thirty years. Medical costs are going through the roof. Even with Medicare, growing old has become an extremely expensive proposition. And, unfortunately, it's only likely to get worse.

We all need to save. We need to invest. We need to prepare so that we can go into our later years with the confidence that we'll be able to get by comfortably. As the statistics show, this is going to require for most of us a complete change in attitude. Planning will have to become part of the fabric of our financial decisions. We'll need to think about exactly how much we're putting away and how we're allocating that money. We won't be able to passively leave it in some account that gives monthly updates we don't read. We'll need to be interested and active, looking for the right opportunities and the right mix of investments.

It's not going to be especially easy. Many people are overwhelmed by the prospect of taking charge of their financial futures. There's so much to learn—all those acronyms and the occasional piece of math. But as I've already pointed out, you can't trust anyone to do it for you. No one is going to be as concerned about your money as you are. And you're not going to be able to learn what you need by osmosis. You'll need to read and do some studying. You are going to have to *learn to earn,* and if you do, the upside is that you will have a potentially *very* rich and very rewarding retirement.

To put it concisely, you need to get active. You need to take charge. You need to stop procrastinating. I don't care if you are twenty-one, or you're sixty-one. You need to get *pumped,* and you need to Rule Your Freakin' Retirement!

The Structure of This Book

This book isn't the only resource you'll need to get your retirement planning on the right track. Sorry, but there's a lot to learn, and there are tons of things that can't be covered in a single volume. My goal in this book is to get you on the right track by giving you a background in the fundamentals. After reading this book, you should have the expertise to look at mutual fund reports and stock charts and know how to digest the information you're seeing. You'll be able to look at the trading activity for a particular stock over a day or week or a few months and be able to see the profitable opportunities that passed; more to the point, you'll be able to look for profitable opportunities in the near future. You'll look at a mutual fund report and say, "Yeah, the numbers look good, but this one's clearly a loser."

That's the goal. And here's how we're going to get there.

Part I: Ruling Today, Preparing to Rule Tomorrow

In this part, you're going to take a hard look at your current situation and your needs in the future. We'll look at your current budget and see where improvements can be made. We'll look at how different savings and investment plans will prepare you for retirement. We'll also look at how various financial burdens will be handled in the quest for a sound retirement.

Part II: Mastering the Tools

There's an alphabet soup of acronyms and references to sections of the tax code in the world of retirement planning. It can be intimidating and confusing when you have to learn about the different types of accounts and funds, along with their expected rates of return and tax advantages. In part II, we'll dive headfirst into the deep end, and you'll learn about all the types of accounts that are available to you, and their tax advantages. We'll also cover all you need to know about bond and stock funds. By the time you're done with this part, you should have a great understanding of where and how your money can be invested.

Part III: Making the Most of It

In part III, you'll see a couple of ways to build on your retirement assets. We'll look at the standard method for investing that is recommended by most financial planners. Then we'll look at the Waxie—that's me—way. And you'll see how learning some basic trends can be crucial in providing you with a comfortable retirement.

Let's get started!

Part I

Ruling Today, Preparing to Rule Tomorrow

....

Chapter 1

An Honest Assessment

....

Credit crisis, housing crisis, banking crisis, oil rising, dollar crushed, people starving, job market sucks, an average American has more debt than worth. There's a food shortage, a water shortage, and there's always the chance of some sort of natural or other disaster. *Help! Help! What am I gonna dooooooo?* And, how am I gonna deal with all that *and* deal with retirement? Are you kidding me? What's up wit dat, Michael "Waxie" Parness?

Okay, first off, calm down and take the proverbial deep breath. I hear ya, and I feel your pain and your fear. Trust me, I have some myself. It's hard to live in this world and feel secure. Even those of you who are financially secure know it's not a bed of roses out there (wherever "there" is!). There are more ways to live in fear than fear itself, by golly! Fear can be self-fulfilling, and so now that I know you have taken that deep breath, you can relax for a moment and realize that even though all those fearful things may on some level ring true, ultimately we still need to move forward with our lives. Part of moving forward means living "as if" the sky isn't going to fall down. Remember, the sky only falls once, and if it does, then none of us will have to worry about anything other than how the hell to get the dang sky off ourselves!

So, let's be honest, shall we? Let's be honest that if you're reading this book, then chances are you are in need of some kind of game plan for your retirement. Chances are you are at least thinking that the sky isn't falling today and that the world isn't ending quite yet. So, given that, let's really look hard, and again honestly, at ways in which we can access our current financial position and move forward toward a happy, healthy, and financially secure retirement. Or come as close as possible to all of the above. Nothing is gonna be perfect, but everything in life, I believe, is a step toward life, or death, and by picking up this book I believe you have taken a nice big step toward Ruling Your Freakin' Retirement!

Let's begin. The hard work is behind us; the rest is just creating a plan for success!

I'm going to start this chapter by presenting a pretty sobering thought: Most of the people reading this book are going to need between $2 million and $5 million if they're going to retire comfortably. Of course, there are all kinds of variables that go into this sort of calculation, and you might need a good deal less or a good deal more. If you plan on living in New York City, as I do, you'll need a lot more income in your retirement than someone living in, for example, Alabama. It also depends on the lifestyle you plan to lead while in retirement. An avid traveler who plans to tour the world will need more than someone who plans to stay closer to home and immerse himself in model building. Moreover, some of you will have pension plans or other sources of income to pull from, which will greatly affect your savings needs. We'll get into the specifics of what you'll actually need in chapter 3.

For the moment, though, let's stick with that $2 to $5 million number, and let's not look at those numbers as daunting. Some of us may or may not even make that work, but we need to set the bar high. I think when you get done with this book you will have a fairly clear path toward maximizing your potential, and that's really all any of us can ask, right? So, again, let's use the $2 to $5 million number because it's going to be applicable for a lot of people. We'll get into details later, but if your annual family income is between $60,000 and $150,000, you'll probably want to be in this range.

That's a lot of money! If you're like most people, you haven't done nearly enough to ensure that you'll have this kind of cash available. If you're like most, you haven't saved enough, you haven't thought enough about your finances, and you haven't educated yourself enough. If this describes you, you're not alone. Not by a long shot. In 2007, the U.S. Census Bureau announced that nearly one in four Americans (23 percent) between the ages of 65 and 74 were still in the workforce. The Census didn't say how many were working by choice and how many were working out of necessity, but we can be pretty sure that many people are in jobs because of a lack of planning, particularly given the state of the Union, our Union!

I don't want to sound like I'm all doom and gloom. As I stated earlier, I think being honest with yourself is being realistic with yourself and is part of your overall retirement plan. I don't want to scare you by pointing to a dire future: That's a state of mind you need to avoid. And I certainly don't want to scold you for being lazy up till now. That's not me. I'm sure you can tell I'm really a *mellow* guy—well, maybe "mellow" isn't the right word—but I am the live-and-let-live sort. What's more, I don't believe in bitching at people to motivate them. I've been bitched at like everyone else, and, honestly, no one is harder on me then me. I find that a lot of people are like that, so the last thing we need is to feel put-down. Trust me, most of what I teach is based on failures I've had. Pain is a great motivator, maybe the best. I've learned from those experiences of pain one thing, that when I'm getting bitched at I'll normally do the absolute minimum that's necessary to quiet the person who is annoying the hell out of me.

So, I don't want to nag and pester and frighten you. No. I want to get you *psyched* to take on retirement. So let me get into my football-coach-at-halftime mode now and do my best to get you inspired for the task ahead. There are few potentially inspiring points I want to cover. Try to keep these in mind when you're feeling bored or annoyed by this task.

- *You're up to it.* You can do this. I'm sure of it. At first this whole topic might seem like a mess of foreign terms, abbreviations, and nasty tax-related things. And to an extent it is. But it's not an overwhelming amount of information. *You can get your head around this!* You just need to break things down into digestible chunks. The concepts aren't hard; it just takes some time and perseverance. And like everything in life, take what you need and leave the rest behind! If you feel more confident with one concept than another, then by all means trust your instincts. It is, after all, *your* money and *your* retirement. I'm just here to hopefully help you *rule* it!

- *You have to be up to it.* Retirement is coming. At least you hope it is, cuz the alternative kind of sucks. Closing your eyes and hoping it will take care of itself isn't going to get you anywhere. So take the challenge of getting your finances together head-on. Go at it like you would an oncoming linebacker, or a tough crossword puzzle, or whatever gets your competitive juices flowing.

- *Doing it right will make you very happy one day.* I'm not necessarily a guy that appreciates delayed gratification. I've been told I'm like a big kid. A six-foot-four kid: I want that ice cream *now!* Before I eat my green beans. But boy-oh-boy, the whole idea of saving and being fiscally smart toward retirement sounds like a worthwhile goal when I think about the things I'll be able to do if I do it right and I'm diligent. I'll be able to pay for my two daughters' weddings, eat in nice restaurants, keep season tickets to the Nets (I may not want them even if I can afford them, mind you). That keeps me looking into the future.

- *Mastery is fun.* Sure, some of the stuff in this book is tedious. I'm not going to try to convince you otherwise. Anyone who reads more than a dozen pages on bonds is going to get sleepy. I do. The subject's better than the best sleeping pills at times. But it's my hope that when you're done reading this, you'll have the baseline knowledge that will allow you to move on and get a ton out of other sources. Maybe one day in the next couple of years, as you grow used to managing your retirement money, you'll discover something that's great for your situation. You'll get a huge rush, because you'll know that all your dedication will have paid off. You'll feel smart and in control. Then you'll be *ruling* your own freakin' retirement, baby.

Now, go out there, because this team's going to State!

Actually, we're not ready for any competition at all—*yet!* As coach, I'd be a fool if I sent you out there without understanding what my team's strengths and weaknesses were. Before we can talk about technical stuff, you'll need to have a good understanding of your current financial position. If you don't know where you are right now, it's going to be pretty well impossible to plan for the future.

Defining Assets

We're going to get a baseline of where you are today by looking at your current net worth. This isn't brain surgery. It should take about five minutes once you have all the needed documents at hand. For starters, you're going to need to get the paperwork on every account that affects your net worth—every checking, savings, and credit card account, including store cards and Christmas and Hanukkah funds. If you have an IRA or a 401(k), get out your most recent report from that as well.

Now, with all this information in hand, get out a piece of paper or fire up a spreadsheet and start entering your numbers. A typical spreadsheet that includes your assets may look something like Table 1-1.

TABLE 1-1. SAMPLE ASSETS TABLE

ACCOUNT	AMOUNT
Checking Account	$1,247
Savings Account	$3,475
Christmas Gifts Act	$465
401(k)	$9,875
IRA	$7,755
TOTAL:	$22,817

Of course, depending on your age and the discipline you've shown in your financial management and your age, you may have a whole lot more in the way of accounts to note here. You may have millions more, or you may have close to nothing. Whatever the case, I want you to boil it down to this—a stark number based on an extremely simple calculation.

At first you may think that this calculation is too simple. It's possible that you're looking at this list of assets and saying, "Whoa, dude. This isn't an accurate picture of my financial situation. I've got way more stuff than this. I'm in much better shape for retirement. I own a house, I've bought my wife great jewelry, and I own a bunch of cool and expensive stuff. Just look at my snazzy car and that big-screen TV. I already rule da world."

Yeah, okay, calm down, big fella, or gella. That stuff may be great, but, really, how helpful are most of those things when it comes to living in retirement? Take the jewelry, for starters. You may have a $7,000 hunk of ice sitting on your wife's finger, but you'd have to be pretty desperate to sell it off so you can live out your golden years. I'm no Dr. Phil, but, trust me, those years aren't going to be so golden if the missus is asked to cash in the most important gift she's ever received so you can pay the rent.

Stereos and electronics and cars are totally worthless when it comes to your retirement. And by the time you're done with your car, it's probably going to have a few dollars' worth of value on trade-in. It sure as heck is not accruing any value as you drive it!

Real estate is to an extent a different matter, and it may be worth including some real estate in this calculation. The thing to keep in my mind about property is that, in some cases, it's a lot like the engagement ring I just mentioned. You can't just sell your house for cash and start living off the proceeds. You and your family need to live somewhere, and if you're like most Americans, you've got a deep emotional attachment to your house. And if the last few years has taught us anything, it's that like every other "asset" it don't always go in a straight line up in value!

Furthermore, even if that were the case, it's difficult to know how gains in real estate are going to aid you in retirement. Say you live in a place where the real estate market has gone crazy, like northern California around Silicon Valley. Over ten years your house may have tripled or quadrupled in value—and that's great. But if you love life in that area (as I love life in New York) and wish to live there in your retirement, you'll never touch the hundreds of thousands in profits you've gained. You may be able to cash out significant sums if and when you downsize. But your new place will also be in that same market. Everything around you is going to be brutally expensive as well.

To actually realize the profit from that real estate, you'll need to move to a cheaper area of the country, or rent instead of own. If you're willing or even eager to make this kind of move, then go ahead and make some kind of calculation that speaks to your net worth. Take a look at the equity in your house and the prices or rents of houses in the markets you're considering. But be conservative when you draw up a value for your real estate gains. Selling and moving are really, really expensive. And this is one place where you want to be conservative.

....

WAXIE'S NOTE: The Value of a House

In this section it may sound like I'm skeptical of the value of owning property. That's not the case. Property has been a solid investment for many
who have put their money in it. Furthermore, home ownership has serious tax advantages over renting—mortgage interest is tax-deductible.
But perhaps the greatest benefit of home ownership, when it comes to
retirement, is the fact that you can pay off a mortgage. Hopefully, by the
time you're in your sixties or seventies, you'll own your place outright.
One of the largest items in your monthly budget will disappear. Besides,
as mentioned above, we don't want to be counting on any market con-
tinually going up. That's an assumption that will make us lazy and perhaps come back to haunt us later if it turns out that we were overly
optimistic. Secondary properties—those that you've bought to sell for a
profit—should definitely be included in your calculation of assets. Make
the best quick estimation you can as to what you stand to gain should
you sell the property, minus fees and taxes.

Defining Liabilities

Now it's time to look carefully at your debts. For most people, debts
will come in two forms, credit cards (including store cards) and
loans. Include college and auto loans, but don't include the mortgage
for your primary residence (because we didn't include the value of
your property when considering assets). Do include mortgage obligations for secondary or investment properties.

WAXIE'S TIP:

**Make sure you're including all of your credit card debt. It's a good time to
check your credit report to see that you don't have any debts you've forgotten
about. By federal law, the major credit agencies are required to give you a copy**

of your credit report for free once a year. Go to AnnualCreditReport.com, and you can check Experian, Equifax, and TransUnion in about fifteen minutes.

Hopefully your list of liabilities is short and the amounts are small. A typical list might look something like this:

TABLE 1-2. SAMPLE LIABILITIES

ACCOUNT	AMOUNT
MasterCard	$875
J.Crew	$250
Auto Loan	$4,000
College Loan	$9,255
TOTAL	$14,380

Now subtract the liabilities from the assets and you'll have a pretty accurate view of the money you currently have available for your retirement.

With the examples taken from Tables 1-1 and 1-2, I'd have total savings of $8,437.

A Closer Look at Your Debts

When looking at your debts, you should differentiate between two types of debt: reasonable debt and *nutso-insane* debt. What I'm calling reasonable debt is usually loans you've taken for some long-term or vital purpose. Student loans would be an excellent example. You also might have taken an auto loan for a car you can afford, which is fine. This sort of debt is pretty much unavoidable for most people, and, in fact, this sort of debt can be viewed as a worthwhile investment. After all, your earning power wouldn't be nearly what it is without that college education. And without a car you might have no choice but to stuff envelopes at home, which probably doesn't pay as well as your current job.

As of the writing of this book, published auto loan rates were in the neighborhood of 6.5 percent. Student loans were usually around 5.0–6.5 percent, though either of these numbers could vary a great deal. While any interest is more than you're happy paying, these sort of rates aren't going to crush you. Your investment accounts should be earning about this or better, so you're not suffering a net loss by maintaining an auto loan or student loans.

Nutso-insane debt is my catchy term for credit card debt. Credit cards routinely charge 12, 18, 20, or even 21 percent interest on out-standing bills. If you have outstanding balances on your credit cards, there is nothing you can do for your overall financial health, which includes your retirement planning, that is better than paying down your credit cards to zero. Your short-term aim should be to get your credit cards to a point where you have no balance and you're paying off the full amount every month.

There's no point in contributing to retirement accounts like IRAs or 401(k)s while you're carrying such high-interest debt. The most you can realistically hope for in an IRA is 9 to 10 percent, in many cases. You don't need to be a financial genius to see that you're suffering a huge net loss if you pay 18 percent interest in one account while gaining interest of 7 percent in another.

To give you an idea of the corrosive nature of credit card debt, think about the following: If you have $8,000 in credit card debt and pay only the minimum of $320 a month, it will take you fourteen years to pay off the full balance, and before you manage to get your balance to zero, you will have paid over $5,000 in interest. Think about that for a second: $5,000 on $8,000 in purchases. That should really put some spending choices in perspective (and cut back on your shopping sprees!). Everything within those $8,000 in purchases was 65 percent more expensive than it would have been if you paid for it directly. That $400 MP3 player cost $660. The $1,400 LCD HDTV turned out to be $2,310. *Sick.*

I remember a time, not long ago, when I had a discussion with a smart young woman (Harvard doctor who was dating me—yes, we question her smarts if she was dating me, but that's for another book!) who had way too much credit card debt. We talked for a little while, and she told me that at the same time she maintained a balance on her credit cards, she also had a significant sum of money in her savings account. I asked her why, and she said she wanted to have some savings for a down payment on a home and other things. I counseled her to forget about anything and everything else. Wipe out the savings account and pay down the cards, I said. I tried to explain to her the obvious result of her decisions: She was losing money monthly. If I had had a computer with me, I would have whipped up a quick chart to dramatize the consequences of her folly.

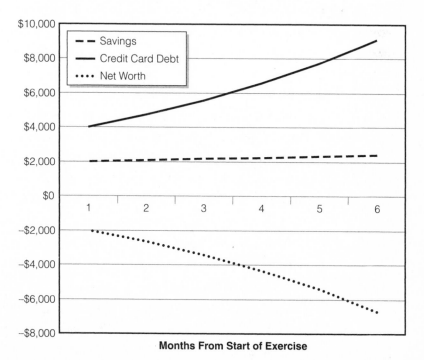

Months From Start of Exercise

Figure 1.1   How credit card debt eats savings

Even if she managed to keep herself from going totally bankrupt, she was still losing tons of money. Her interest rate on her savings account, a mere 4 percent, was getting totally outpaced by her 18 percent credit card rate. As a result, whether she wanted to admit it or not, her net worth was taking a beating.

I wish the course of action had been clearer to her than it was. She needed to forget everything else and start paying off her credit card debt. If you are sitting with balances on high-interest credit cards, nothing is more important than getting rid of those balances. Pull out all the stops to get rid of that debt. Cash out bonds and IRAs, stop contributing to your 401(k), raid any other savings that you have. Borrow from family and friends. Pay all you can till that one's paid off, then work your way down the line. And start with the card that has the highest interest rate.

BOTTOM LINE: I hear a ton of smart people tell me they owe vast sums in credit card debt, but have some savings and ask me what to do. Three words—*Pay it off!* Pronto, period. *Now!*

....
WAXIE'S TIP

There are a lot of scam artists who take advantage of people who are already in substantial debt. Don't sign on to any sort of consolidation loan or debt counseling service before checking them out first. You can get some good, honest advice on dealing with debt from the National Foundation for Credit Counseling: http://www.nfcc.org.

Examining the Total

Let's get back to the net worth calculation that you made by subtracting your liabilities from your assets. That number, more or less, is what you have available for your retirement. How does the number look to you? Does it seem like it's a decent stop along the way to obtaining the two, three, or four million dollars you could need when retirement rolls around?

Just to give you an idea of how your current numbers stack up, Table 1-3 shows you how much you can expect to make on varying amounts of investment over a range of time frames. In the table I'm assuming a pretty conservative return rate of 8 percent per year. Of course, all sorts of assumptions go into these sorts of long-range calculations, and we could argue about the wisdom of assuming an 8 percent return rather than a 9 or 10. But for the sake of baseline planning, let's just assume these numbers are reasonable.

TABLE 1-3. EIGHT PERCENT INTEREST OVER VARYING TIME FRAMES

AMOUNT IN SAVINGS	5 YEARS	10 YEARS	20 YEARS	25 YEARS	30 YEARS
$5,000	$7,347	$10,795	$23,305	$34,242	$50,313
$10,000	$14,693	$21,589	$46,610	$68,485	$100,627
$25,000	$36,733	$53,973	$116,524	$171,212	$251,566
$50,000	$73,466	$107,946	$233,048	$342,424	$503,133
$100,000	$146,933	$215,892	$466,096	$686,848	$1,006,266
$200,000	$293,866	$431,785	$932,191	$1,369,695	$2,012,531
$400,000	$587,731	$863,570	$1,846,383	$2,739,390	$4,025,063

So let's say that you're thirty-five-years old and you're planning on retiring when you're sixty-five. If you have $100,000 in your retirement plan and you contribute nothing else through the years, you'll have only $1 million when it comes time to retire. As I said before, you're probably going to need at least double that. So you've got some work ahead of you.

Age and Money

The next portion of this assessment is quite a bit easier than the first. All it requires is that you go into your wallet and pull out your driver's license. From there, look at your date of birth and figure out how old you are. Write your age down somewhere: This is the age at which you're going to get serious about your retirement planning.

The importance of starting now cannot be exaggerated. Go back to Table 1-3 and look at the numbers. They're remarkable. Look at how dramatically your money will work for you if you start young. Every dollar you have saved at age 35 will be worth ten dollars at age 65. If you can get some money socked away while you're in your twenties and thirties you'll be much better off than if you try to get yourself set while you're only ten or fifteen years away from your retirement and your money has less time to work for you.

When you start early, the money you have has an opportunity to *compound.* You gain interest in one year, and the next year the previ-

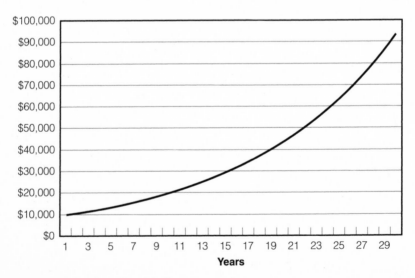

Figure 1.2   The miracle of compound interest

ous year's principal *and* the interest gain yet more interest. Just look at what will happen to $10,000 over thirty years if it collects 8 percent interest per year.

Starting now, as you can see, will have tremendous rewards down the road.

Big and Small Measures

Right now, you may be feeling pretty darn good about where you stand, or you may be feeling kind of crappy. Most people I know vacillate between the two extremes. I know I have that tendency at times, so you are not alone if that describes you. Those of you in the former category—you who have some money but know you're going to need more—may only have small changes to make. You'll need to save a little more diligently or invest with a little more savvy. In fact, everyone who picks up this book should start thinking right now about the small measures that will make a monumental difference. Think about it this way: Moving some money from one mutual fund to another that is 99 percent identical could save you $100,000 over twenty years. Learning a relatively simple trading technique could net you another $100,000 over the years. Hell, giving up on your daily latte or brown-bagging your lunch to work could add tens of thousands over a long time horizon.

Sweating the details and making small changes are huge in retirement planning. This is a theme I'll be returning to again and again.

Unfortunately, there are going to be some people who are reading this book who are looking at the numbers of their net worth and their time horizon and are realizing that they're in a bad spot.

If this is you, realize, first off, that you're not alone. Second, and more important, there are still things you can do. The work is going to be harder for you, of course. You may have to scale back on some expectations. But that's okay. Once you come to a realistic sense of what you can and can't do, you'll Rule Your Freakin' Retirement!

Quiz

1. **Which of the items below are *NOT* appropriate to include in a calculation of net assets?**

   a. Current value of primary home

   b. Value of automobiles

   c. Realized profit on a secondary property

   d. Auction value of prized family heirloom

   Answer: a, b, d

2. **Which of the following are *NOT* appropriate to include in a calculation of net liabilities?**

   a. College loan debt

   b. Store card debt

   c. Primary residence mortgage debt

   d. Secondary residence mortgage debt

   Answer: c

3. **Which of the following is the most important short-term financial planning goal?**

   a. Paying off credit cards

   b. Putting money into a 401(k)

   c. Buying a house

   d. Paying off student loans

   Answer: a

4. **Starting retirement savings early allows you to take advantage of what concept that assures your money will grow?**

   a. Compounding

   b. Accrual

   c. Allocation growth

   d. Net growth

   Answer: a

5. **Which credit card should you pay off first?**

    a. Store card with 12 percent interest rate and $1,000 balance

    b. Credit card with 18 percent rate and $2,000 balance

    c. Credit card with 16 percent rate and $4,000 balance

    Answer: b. Always pay off the card having the highest interest rate first

Chapter 2

Your Needs Now and in Retirement

If you're anything like me, there's going to come a time in the not too distant future when you actually enjoy the work of retirement planning. There's no way I could have said that before my two girls were born. I'm a fly-by-the-seat-of-my-pants personality type. I don't even like to plan tomorrow most of the time, but with kids I've learned to be responsible, at least part of the time. And I'm now not just planning for my retirement, I'm planning for their futures as well. That's been a helluva incentive to take this stuff seriously, so seriously I can now pass some of it on to you. By developing your own retirement plan, you'll gain a good understanding of the investment tools available to you as well as the savvy to use these tools properly. Even when you stumble across something you've never heard of before, you'll feel great—empowered—when it takes you only a short time to figure this new thing out. Knowledge is power, and being smart and powerful is fun, and could lead to a "phat" retirement!

Right now we're only in chapter 2, and the fun has just begun. More—*much more*—is ahead of us. Before you can wrap your mind around funds and options and bonds and annuities, you need to have control of the basic math of your current financial picture. You need to have a solid understanding of your current expenses and your likely expenses in the future.

You need a budget for both today and your upcoming retirement. Yes, there is that dreaded B word—"budget"! Take it from me, it'll be well worth the time, the effort, and the, at times, anxiety. The goal is to lift all the bad stuff away, and not knowing is what creates most fear. A lot of kids fear the dark; we adults often have similar fears of what's lurking behind the employment door, the economy door, the terrorism door, the marriage door, and so on. Many of these fears are out of our control. There's only so much in life we truly can control, so taking charge of those areas where we can usually alleviates a lot of stress.

These budgets should be highly ambitious, yet totally realistic. That is, you should budget so that you can live as comfortably and happily as is practical while you're retired. Your retirement should not be about downsizing—quite the contrary, in my view. You should be comfortable in your retirement, not stressed out trying to figure out what to sell on eBay in order to live the longest, richest life possible. That's the ambitious part. You also need to be totally realistic in seeing how you're going to get there. As I've already mentioned, you need money—a lot of it. To get the money you need, you'll have to budget practically and save. Yes, that other dreaded word for many of us, the S word—"save"!

Before we move on to talk about budgets of today and tomorrow, I'm going to return to a point I made emphatically in the previous chapter. No budget and no savings plan will make a lick of sense if you're flushing money down the toilet in credit card debt. If you have a current balance, you need to do everything possible to pay it off. Furthermore, if you want to buy something, you can't view credit card debt as an option. You may be dying to get that $1,400 big-screen TV, and that's fine. But budget for it and save for it and pay for it with your debit card or a check when you're able. Paying more in interest on your credit cards than you are accruing in your savings account (or brokerage account) is downright foolish, and can be fatal to your retirement.

WAXIE'S NOTE: Sh*t Happens

Life often throws us nasty curveballs. There are true emergencies and situations that can require immediate action and taking on immediate, potentially high-interest, debt. Just make sure you're not confusing an aching desire for an urgent need. Looking after the health and well-being of a close friend or relative is, of course, a perfectly good reason to go into debt. Upgrading to a ruby-studded cell phone is not.

Your Monthly Budget

Now it's time to take a hard look at the money you have coming in and the money that's heading out.

There are a couple of ways you can go about getting the most accurate view of your current spending activities. You can use software, such as Quicken (http://www.quicken.com), into which you can download credit card and banking activities. The software will then give you nice graphs and charts showing exactly where your dollars are spent. A lot of people abandon financial software after a time: They just don't want to deal with it. But if you think using computer tracking for a few months will really help you get a handle on your budget, use it, even if you think you're not going to use it forever. Alternatively, you can fire up a spreadsheet and let it do the addition and subtraction for you. There are plenty of budget templates for Excel online that you can start with. Or if you want to go old school, you can go with a pencil and paper and maybe a calculator.

It doesn't matter what you use, as long as you're thorough and brutally honest. This is one area of your life where you need to be accurate. You can't plan if you don't have your budgetary house in order.

Table 2-1 shows the categories and line items you should include in your budget.

● ● ● ● ● ● ● ● ● ● ● ● ● ● ● ● ● ●
WAXIE'S TIPS

The important thing is that the budget should work for you. Some line items in Table 2-1 could belong in categories other than the ones they're listed in. For example, I have auto insurance under the Transportation category, and health insurance in the Well-being category. If it's easier for you to have an Insurance category, play with the sheet.

● ● ● ● ● ● ● ● ● ● ● ● ● ● ● ● ●

When figuring a monthly budget, there are items that are easy to leave out or underestimate. For example, you might think, "Oh, I don't have any car repair costs this month," and leave it blank. But you know full well that you're likely to spend several hundred over the year on your car(s)—and that's if nothing goes terribly wrong. (If you live in a place like New York City, where there are taxicabs, you'll spend more no matter how good a driver you are.) It's important to make your best estimates of these items. Make the same sort of estimations for your travel budget as well. Again, this is an area where you want to be liberal in your estimates. Better to have an overage than be so conservative in your budget that you have a shortfall.

TABLE 2-1. MONTHLY BUDGET

ITEM	AMOUNT
TAXES	
Federal	_____
State/Local	_____
FICA	_____
Other	_____

(continued)

TABLE 2-1. **MONTHLY BUDGET** (*continued*)

ITEM	AMOUNT
HOUSING	
Rent/Mortgage	_____
Property insurance	_____
Property taxes	_____
UTILITIES	
Oil/gas	_____
Water	_____
Garbage	_____
Phone/Internet	_____
Cable/Internet	_____
Cell phone	_____
HOUSEHOLD SERVICES	
Landscaping/Gardening	_____
Pool	_____
Other	_____
LOAN PAYMENTS	
Education	_____
Credit/Store cards	_____
TRANSPORTATION	
Loans	_____
Mass transit	_____
Gasoline	_____
Parking/Tolls	_____
Maintenance	_____
WELL-BEING	
Health insurance	_____
Co-pays	_____

ITEM	AMOUNT
Prescription medication	_____
Gym membership	_____
Other	_____
PET	
Food/Toys	_____
Vet	_____
Boarding	_____
CHILDREN	
Day care/Babysitting	_____
Toys/Misc.	_____
Allowance	_____
Child support	_____
FOOD	
Groceries	_____
Ordering in	_____
Work lunch/Coffee	_____
ENTERTAINMENT	
Tickets (movie, theater, music)	_____
Vacation/Travel	_____
Gambling	_____
EDUCATION	
Tuition	_____
Books/Materials	_____
Beauty	_____
Hair	_____
Nails	_____

(continued)

TABLE 2-1. MONTHLY BUDGET (*continued*)

ITEM	AMOUNT
CLOTHING	
Adults	_____
Children	_____
PROFESSIONAL ASSISTANCE	
Lawyer	_____
Accountant	_____
OTHER INSURANCE	
Renters insurance	_____
Disability	_____
Liability	_____
Other	_____
SAVINGS	
IRA	_____
Emergency fund	_____
Home down payment	_____
Specialty purchase	_____
Other	_____

Examining Your Budget

Once you've gone through your budget, you should be looking to it as a sort of wake-up call. Most people should be saving *at least* 10 percent of their gross income and putting it into various retirement accounts. If you're not doing that—or even if you are—you need to look at this budget and see where you can do a better job of cutting back on excesses and adding to your savings and retirement accounts.

....
WAXIE'S TIP

Some of you may be like me: You can afford certain luxuries, and even take for granted things like first-class travel or eating at the finest restaurants. Think about this: If you cut back these things even *slightly,* you will have significant savings. You like to fly first-class? Who doesn't? But do you really need to do so for that two-hour trip from New York City to Atlanta? Probably not. I've found that cutting back even a little can expand my retirement accounts in a huge way each year. I did an interview on *Good Day NY* a couple of years ago and that's exactly what I spoke about. I now only fly first-class if it's at least a five-hour trip or it's a redeye and I need to sleep. I'm a big guy, and I am anything but cheap, but I also hate wasting money.

Most Americans have a few areas where they can do much, much better in terms of savings, places where they can tighten their belts a little without feeling any significant discomfort. For starters, look at how you're spending your cash on things like espresso drinks and lunch. Eating out and ordering in too frequently are also common money sucks. Spend seven dollars a day on lunch and a couple on coffee, and you're talking serious money: about $160 per month, or nearly $2,000 per year. Thirty years from now, if invested properly, that $2,000 will balloon to $20,000.

Save another $100 a month by cooking rather than ordering in. Keep another $50 by forgoing some brand-name clothes.

The point is that you can make changes that add significantly to your bottom line and give you a leg up on the ladder to retirement without compromising anything noticeable in your lifestyle. The following example offers a great illustration.

I have a friend named Jon who has a weakness for good cigars. Generally, Jon smokes one cigar a day. This annoys his wife and gives his clothing a horrid smell, and makes him, according to her, "unkissable," but that's not important now, particularly to me, since I would never kiss the dude! The health effects of this habit are also troubling, but forget that for the time being. So Jon smokes one $7 cigar a day, pretty much every day. It's a luxury he enjoys and feels he can afford. For the sake of his retirement, I'm not suggesting that Jon live like a monk. If he wants to continue to indulge like this, that's fine. But what if he were to cut back and smoke just twice a week. It wouldn't really affect his lifestyle in any meaningful way (heck, he might enjoy the cigars he does smoke even more) and he'd save $21 per week (the $35 he had been spending per week minus the $14 he'd spend at twice per week). Saving $21 per week for 52 weeks, leads to an annual savings of $1,092. Not bad.

But the really remarkable savings start coming when you look at what happens over the decades. Jon is thirty-five years old, and from this vantage, he thinks that he'll work another thirty years. How much will he save over that period of time? You need to make a couple of assumptions to come up with a number. Assuming that cigar prices rise

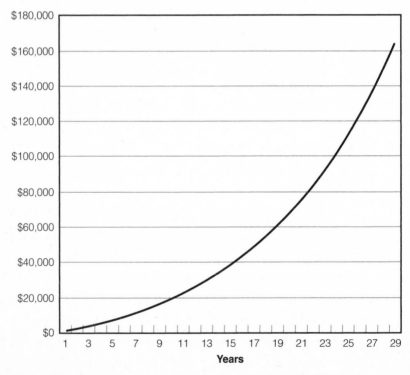

Figure 2.1 How saving weekly cigar money multiplies

with a normal rate of inflation, say 3 percent, and that the money he saves every year manages an average annual return of 8 percent, he'd put some serious cash away. Figure 2.1 shows what he could expect.

In thirty years, he'd have over $160,000 more saved for retirement than he otherwise would. What did he need to do to pull off this remarkable savings? Cut back slightly on a disgusting habit. Here again you can see the amazing effect that compounding has on long-term investments.

Travel and vacation are other common areas where cutting back is natural and relatively easy.

When Small Steps Won't Cut It

There are some people for whom this budget process will reveal something pretty scary: They have essentially no place to cut back. They find that between their mortgage, health care, groceries, and taxes that there's pretty close to nothing left. Nothing for vacation, nothing for dinners out, nothing for the IRA.

If you find that you're in this boat, or you can't see a way that you'll be able to save at least 10 percent of your gross income, it's time to look hard and long at the big-ticket items on your budget— your mortgage or rent and your car payments. A lot of people have spent way too much on their homes. So much that they're now essentially broke because all their money is going into the mortgage.

Often there are two sorts of justifications for this state of affairs: (1) It's our home, and we deserve the nicest thing we can manage; and (2) It's a great investment.

There are a couple of big problems with these justifications. For starters, if you can't manage any savings because of your mortgage, you're almost certainly performing a dangerous trapeze act without a net. You're one setback—a short period of unemployment, an illness— away from losing everything. Foreclosures happen at alarming rates in this country (and have reached historic heights in 2008!) because people consistently overextend themselves. If you're in that boat, you need to do what you can to get out. I know it's psychologically brutal, I've been there; but if you need to downsize or move to a more affordable neighborhood, that's what you need to do. It's not the end of the world, even if it feels that way. Life truly is about going with the flow and accepting life on its terms. Martial artists learn that by rolling with a punch they can then counterpunch with force. Selling your home now may allow you to buy it back later at a cheaper price! Ya never know, ya never know. My experience is that it usually works out for the best if you allow it to.

WAXIE'S SIDEBAR:
The Credit Crunch of 2007–08 and After

The stock market went bonkers in the summer of 2008. There were wild swings in the market daily. Many investors and hedge funds lost a fair amount of money as some stocks and many other investment vehicles lost value. The reason for this unrest: foreclosures. Lending companies had been giving outsized mortgages to people who couldn't possibly afford them. Adjustable rate mortgages (ARMs) and other short-term credit mortgage facilities created a proverbial glass house. It had to break at some point. One thing I know from trading in the stock market for years is that *nothing* goes in a straight line, and nothing always goes *up!* Real estate included. All those people bought into the notion that real estate must keep going up. Like everything else, when everyone is bullish, there are no more buyers and "what goes up—must come down!" These people bought into the American dream—the big house for their family—without looking clearly at whether they could afford the reality. Many couldn't, and the companies who made the loans got hurt badly. Many things in the markets are interrelated, and the problems in the mortgage market ended up affecting almost every sector of the global economy. I'll talk a little more about the mortgage mess in the chapter on bonds.

Please don't be seduced by the idea that putting all your money in your home is okay because it's a great investment. As I already mentioned, the quality of the investment might be overrated because you may not have a whole lot of profit to spend if you want to stay in the house or the area. Moreover, one of the more important concepts in retirement planning is diversification. You want your money in a lot of different pots—domestic stocks, international stocks, bonds, money market funds, and many other things we'll talk about throughout this book. Diversification protects you from a downturn in any one segment. Remember that real estate is just one segment of the investment marketplace.

While real estate has shown astonishing appreciation in prices over the past couple of decades, as I write this book, the country is in the midst of a horrid housing slump. Prices are down 50 percent or more in some parts of the country. When will it recover? How will growth in prices be after the recovery? I have no idea. Nor does anyone else. Frankly, I think it'll get worse before it gets better, but either way I'm not in the crystal ball business, and neither are you. As I always say to my clients at trendfund.com in the stock market, at some point the market doesn't come back. Look at the NASDAQ. Even after a huge rally in the last few years, it's still, as I write this, about 65 percent lower than it was at its peak in 2000. The same happens in every market. Never assume, because, as you know, when you assume you make an *ass* out of—*you* (and not me!).

Budget for Now and the Future

In chapter 1 I said that you'd likely need between two and five million dollars to retire properly. (Has that number ceased to shock you yet?) But to get a more specific idea of what you and your family will need, you have to stop and contemplate the life you're hoping to live. You need to have a rough budget for yourself in retirement. The budget for the future may be quite different from the one you keep today.

To show how things change, I'm going to build a fictional example: the Jones family. Here's a little bit about them:

THE JONES FAMILY

NAMES: John and Jane Jones. Kids, Jimmy and Janice (10, 7)
LOCATION: Suburb of a major city
AGE: Late thirties
COMBINED INCOME: $75,000 ($6,250/month, pretax)
LIVING ARRANGEMENT: Three-bedroom house; they're seven years into a 30-year mortgage
CARS: 2; one 2 years old; the other is a junker
DEBTS: John has $11,000 remaining in student loans
SCHOOLING OF KIDS: Both children go to public schools
HEALTH INSURANCE: Through John's teaching job, they have good health insurance for the family

Table 2-2 shows the highlights of the Joneses' budget. It's not thorough, but gives an idea of how a couple of reasonably responsible people have structured their finances.

TABLE 2-2. JONES SUMMARY MONTHLY BUDGET IN 2008

ITEM	AMOUNT
Fed/State/Local taxes	$1,100
Mortgage/Property tax/Home owner's ins.	$1,700
Home upkeep	$275
Car payments	$400
Student loans	$235
Groceries	$450
Utilities	$165
Other auto expenses (gas, repairs)	$250
Vacation	$300
Entertainment	$200

ITEM	AMOUNT
Health/Dental	$175
Retirement savings	$500
TOTAL	$5,750

I know this budget is far from complete. It also may not match what you're experiencing in your own life, but to get that picture you'll have to look at your own budget carefully. The point here is to show how the Joneses' budget is going to change when they retire in 2032.

TABLE 2-3. JONES SUMMARY MONTHLY BUDGET IN 2032

ITEM	AMOUNT
Fed/State/Local taxes	$700
Property tax/Home owner's ins.	$400
Home upkeep	$325
Car payments	$275
Student loans	$0
Groceries	$300
Utilities	$165
Other auto expenses (gas, repairs)	$250
Vacation	$1,000
Entertainment	$450
Health/Dental	$450
Retirement savings	$0
TOTAL	$4,315

Some things will change for the Joneses in 2032 that will save them a lot of money. They'll have paid off their mortgage, which will save them a sizable amount per month. If they're careful about their savings vehicles, using Roth IRAs and Roth 401(k)s when available, they'll also decrease their tax burden tremendously (more about Roths later). They also won't be saving for retirement, which is a big line item in their 2008 budget. Student loans will be paid off as well.

But there are increases. They can count on spending more on health care as they age. And the Joneses also greatly increased their travel budget: They want to see the world.

Using this simplistic calculation, you can see that the Joneses need about 75 percent of their current income in retirement. This number is pretty typical, actually. Most financial planners recommend that you accumulate somewhere between 75 and 90 percent of your working budget in retirement. So the Joneses need about $50,000 a year. Right away, you may be wondering how that number jives with my claim that they'll need to save millions in order to survive. Well, here's how.

Remember that the numbers in Tables 2-2 and 2-3 ignore inflation. Over the years, the inflation rate varies, but generally it averages about 3 percent a year. If these averages hold, the $50,000 in 2003 will translate to roughly $120,000 in 2036, though the exact number is unknowable.

When you're retired, you'd do best if you were living off the interest of your investments. You don't want to be eating into principal (especially early in your retirement) unless it's absolutely necessary. When you're living off of principal, you want to be in very, very stable investments—like certificates of deposit and bonds. You can generally count on these paying roughly 5 percent interest. To get $120,000 of interest out of your principal, you need $2.4 million earning interest for you.

Table 2-4 shows the effect of 3 percent inflation on $50,000 over the next forty years. Suffice it to say, it sucks! In addition, it shows the principal needed to generate that income, assuming you're earning 5 percent on your investments.

TABLE 2-4. EFFECTS OF INFLATION ON $50,000

YEAR	INFLATION-ADJUSTED AMOUNT	PRINCIPAL NEEDED TO GENERATE INCOME AT 5%
2006	$ 50,000	$ 1,000,000
2011	$ 57,963.70	$ 1,159,274
2016	$ 67,195.82	$ 1,343,916
2021	$ 77,898.37	$ 1,557,967
2026	$ 90,305.56	$ 1,806,111
2031	$ 104,688.90	$ 2,093,778
2036	$ 121,363.12	$ 2,427,262
2041	$ 140,693.12	$ 2,813,862
2046	$ 163,101.89	$ 3,262,038

The Effect of Social Security on Your Budget

Each year the federal government sends you a form detailing what you can expect to receive in Social Security payments when it comes time to retire. The following information, along with numbers that are specific to you, will be on page 2 of the package:

You have earned enough credits to qualify for benefits. At your current earnings rate, if you stop working and start receiving benefits . . .

At age 62, your payment would be about. . . . . $ 975 a month

If you continue working until your full retirement age (67 years), your payment would be about. . . . . $ 1,412 a month

At age 70, your payment would be about. . . . . $ 1,761 a month

Here you see that the Joneses are going to get some decent help in retirement from the government—or, to put it more accurately, they'll be getting some back after decades of paying in. Notice that the amount they will receive changes greatly according to when they chose to retire. These are substantial sums and can have a really big impact on what you'll need to retire. Actually, you need to look beyond the sheet you get from Social Security and do a little more digging before you find out exactly how much you can expect a month.

Now let's look again at the situation the Joneses are in. We thought they might need around $2.4 million to maintain their income. Let's revisit that figure while considering Social Security.

We concluded that the Joneses wanted roughly $50,000 in current dollars, or about $4,200 per month, to live the life they were looking to live in retirement. Assuming that they'll be getting $1,400 from Social Security (actually, the number from a working couple will be higher), they'll only need to generate $2,900 per month (in today's dollars), or roughly $36,000 per year, from their investments (again, we're sticking with current dollar values).

Doing some quick math to take inflation into account, I can see that $36,000 equates to roughly $87,000 in 2036. And to generate $87,000 per year from 5 percent interest on principal, the Joneses would need to have about $1.75 million in savings. Note that without Social Security they would have needed $2.4 million—almost $750,000 more.

The Role of Pensions

Pensions aren't what they used to be in American society. There was a time when industries had pension plans that their workers could count on in retirement. But these days most companies, even massive ones, find them too expensive, and offer 401(k)s and the like instead. Government workers are among the last people on the planet to have access to pensions. Some can be quite generous.

Pensions are so highly variable that's it's difficult to generalize. To get an idea of how your pension might affect your retirement needs, you'll need to talk with the people who make your pension possible. Someone in the human resources office where you work or the benefits administrator at your union should be able to help you out.

Making Your Own Calculation

At this point, it should be pretty clear that there are tons of variables when it comes to determining how much you need for retirement. There's no way around it—you're going to have to look hard at your own situation and that of your family and draw some conclusions as to your financial wants and needs. Spend time with the budget you have now and the budget you think you'll have upon retirement. I hate repeating myself, but I will: Do yourself a favor and be *conservative!* It's better to underestimate than overestimate, for obvious reasons. It'll be great if you have *too much* money, right?

. . . .
WAXIE'S TIP

The Internet is loaded with retirement planning calculators. They may very well be easier to use than the tables I've provided in this section. I particularly like the calculator at Bloomberg.com: http://www.bloomberg.com/invest/calculators/retire.html

Now you can settle down and do some calculations. Have the following numbers handy:

- *Desired monthly retirement budget*
- *Amount expected from Social Security or pension*
- *Years until retirement*

STEP 1. Subtract the amount expected from Social Security from your total desired monthly budget.

STEP 2. Multiply the number derived from step 1 by 12.

STEP 3. Look at the multipliers in Table 2-5. Multiply the number in step 2 by the appropriate number from Table 2-5.

TABLE 2-5.

YEARS UNTIL RETIREMENT	MULTIPLIER
5	1.16
10	1.34
15	1.55
20	1.80
25	2.09
30	2.43

STEP 4. Multiply the number derived from step 3 by 20.

This will give you the total amount you'll need in your retirement account by the time you're ready to stop working.

Stare at the number for a while, and get a drink if you need it. Or if you don't drink, imagine a twelve-step meeting of Retirement Anonymous! Hi, my name is Retiree and I don't want to be broke. Hi, Retiree! Don't worry, the meeting will be packed, you'll have lots of company.

Let's keep going and see if we can keep you from doing either, unless you want to for some odd reason. Who am I to deny you such guilty pleasures! Whatever floats your boat.

Now let's do some quick-and-dirty calculations to see how close you are to reaching that goal. We'll need a few numbers to do the calculations:

■ *Current amount in retirement accounts*
■ *Annual income*

- *Percentage of annual income saved every year*
- *Years until retirement*

STEP 1. Mutiply the amount currently in your retirement accounts by the multipliers in Table 2-6.

TABLE 2-6. MULTIPLIERS FOR CURRENT AMOUNT IN RETIREMENT ACCOUNT

YEARS UNTIL RETIREMENT	MULTIPLIER
5	1.46
10	2.15
15	3.17
20	4.66
25	6.84
30	10.00

STEP 2. Multiply your current salary by your savings rate (e.g., 0.1 for 10 percent) and by the following multipliers.

TABLE 2-7. MULTIPLIERS FOR STEP 2

YEARS UNTIL RETIREMENT	MULTIPLIER
5	8
10	20
15	38
20	68
25	100
30	180

Add the numbers for steps 1 and 2 together and you've got a crude estimate of how much money you'll have available in your accounts when you're ready to retire. Are you close? If not, you need to start looking at your savings rate so that you might get yourself where you need to be.

- -
WAXIE'S NOTE

I want you to go to a variety of Internet calculators to look at how various assumptions in savings rate, rate of return, and budget in retirement affect your savings plan. I've used some very conservative assumptions in creating these tables, and you may be a little happier if you plug in some rosier but still realistic numbers.
- -

How to Save, How Not to Save

There's no getting around the fact that everything related to personal finance—including retirement planning—has a huge emotional and psychological element to it. Finding out that you aren't on a good path is tough, and considering what you may need to do to get on the correct path can be somewhere between sobering and depressing, depending on your outlook. Realizing that you may have been less than entirely responsible for a good portion of your life is no fun either. Realizing that you've seriously screwed up can be devastating.

I mention this now because there's much bad advice out there and many financial predators. I think these "experts" find an audience among so many people who are in bad emotional shape because their financial situation isn't what it should be.

When it comes to financial planning in general or retirement planning in particular, don't let anyone treat you like a child—or an idiot. Keep your senses about you and make sure you're giving everything "the sniff test." I mention this now because, in the realm of bolstering your savings, there are some suggestions you'll see from "financial experts" that you can't get near because they reek.

One concept you see repeatedly is the idea that you should "pay yourself first." Adherents of the pay-yourself-first philosophy say that the first dollar you make should go to retirement savings. Your first dollar, they say, should be put in an IRA, 401(k), or another sort of retirement vehicle. You are to do this before anything else—before you pay your mortgage, your credit cards, or your doctor.

One famous author who preaches pay-yourself-first says this works, whereas budgeting doesn't, because people don't stick to budgets. But if you pay yourself that first dollar, you're sure to be diligent about retirement savings. Or so he says.

If you've been reading what I've said so far in this book, you might guess how I feel about this advice. You're going to pay yourself before you pay down a credit card? Are you kidding me? It's moronic. It's self-destructive. I know it. You know it. This guru certainly knows it. He only offers up this advice because he thinks it's all you're fit to handle. It's idiot-proof advice. The people he advises, therefore, must be idiots.

Give me a break. You want to control your future, get a handle on your financial life; do not create some bizarre house of cards where it seems you're building for retirement while you're actually going broke.

Moreover, the simplicity of paying yourself first makes savings no more foolproof than ordinary budgeting. Think of it this way: You've declared that you'll pay yourself first no matter what. Then a relative gets sick, and you need to do some expensive traveling; then the collection agent calls; then a pipe bursts in your bathroom, flooding the kitchen. Are you going to pay yourself while your kitchen is underwater?

Now, despite my annoyance with some of what's said by the pay-yourself-firsters, there are concepts buried within the philosophy that are worth exploring. For starters, there's no question that you need to make saving a priority. By far the easiest way to do it is to have your employer deduct money from your paycheck so that you can fund a 401(k) or some other retirement plan. As you'll learn later, there are huge tax advantages to funding a 401(k), or even better a Roth

401(k), if available. We'll talk a lot more about these accounts later, but, for sure, you should put every dollar in these accounts that you can.

The other message that's useful to take away from pay-yourself-first is that it encourages regular and consistent savings, whether it is in a 401(k) or elsewhere. This is absolutely the best way to go. You'll put away more if you're diligent, and your money will start earning returns at once.

The point is that you want to be regular and diligent. But you need to be smart as well. Don't save if it's a net loser. But without question, you need to save!

Quiz

1. **How should you budget for the purchase of luxury items?**

    a. Pay with a credit card, then pay off as soon as possible

    b. Take from savings accounts when available

    c. Create a line item in the monthly budget that will allow you to buy the item eventually

    d. Avoid luxury items at all costs

    Answer: c

2. **What is the minimum amount most households should be saving for retirement?**

    a. 5 percent

    b. 10 percent

    c. 15 percent

    d. 20 percent

    Answer: b

3. **Which of the following are common areas where cutbacks in expenditures can lead to significant retirement savings?**

    a. Vacations

    b. Meals

    c. Entertainment

    d. Unhealthy hobbies (smoking, drinking)

    Answer: All of the above

4. *Over the last thirty years, what has been the approximate annual rate of inflation?*

   a. 2 percent

   b. 3 percent

   c. 4 percent

   d. 5 percent

   Answer: b

5. *The philosophy that has you putting money in an IRA before paying down credit cards is known as:*

   a. A stupid plan

   b. Savings before sense

   c. Pay-yourself-first

   d. Save first, go broke later

   Answer: c

Chapter 3

Creating a Profile and Looking Ahead

Are you ready to retire yet? No, I didn't think so. So, read on, dudes and dudesses!

Our first couple of chapters dealt with retirement planning in the abstract. But good retirement preparation is all about doing the right thing at the night time. In trading I tell my clients to: "Plan your trade and trade your plan!" With retirement let's dub it: "Plan your retirement, and enjoy your retirement!" Or something like that. You have to understand the theory and *then* make the correct decisions for your own life and your own situations. To that end, for this chapter, I thought it would be helpful to look at the financial profiles of some people at different stages of their lives. By looking at these profiles, we'll get a feel for the challenges they face. This kind of view is really important because, let's face it, retirement is just one of a number of financial pressures you'll encounter in your life.

In fact, good retirement planning is largely about meeting these other challenges soberly. For starters, you need to realize that when you're married and have kids, your retirement is not just your own, it's your family's. While you're planning, you need to be prepared for contingencies. You'll need to ask the big what-ifs. What if you get terribly sick? What if there's a Mack truck out there with your name on it? If any of these horrible things happen, will your spouse and kids be able to carry on without sacrificing too large a portion of their standard of living?

Profiles

None of these profiles may fit your current situation, exactly, but there should be enough commonalities between you and the profiled people that you'll take away some useful concepts.

JUST-WORKING JACK

NAME: Jack Jones
AGE: 24
CAREER STAGE: Early. Two years out of college, Jack is enjoying his first salaried position. Jack has a number of promotions in his future.
MARITAL STATUS: Single, and loving it
CHILDREN: None
LIVING SITUATION: Apartment, shared with a friend
SALARY: $37,000
CURRENT RETIREMENT SAVINGS: $0
MAJOR OBLIGATIONS: $12,000 student loans; $14,000 car loan
MAJOR UPCOMING EXPENSES: Cancún trip

Ah, youth. Jack has most of his life and career ahead of him. He's not making a ton of money, but he feels quite wealthy. And why shouldn't he? Outside of his rent and his car and student loans, he's got essentially no big financial obligations at all—no insurance, no mortgage. Discretionary spending consumes a lot of Jack's paychecks. He buys more than his share of rounds, and when he goes out with women he's a generous date. Jack is starting to find living with a roommate a little trying, but otherwise life is pretty good.

Let's face it, Jack's not thinking about retirement. If I carried this book to him and shoved it into his hands, he wouldn't crack the cover. Really, that would be fine, because I wouldn't have a whole lot to say to Jack. I'm not about to tell a twenty-four-year-old to be less extravagant on dates. If he were listening, these are the only suggestions I would make that I think Jack might actually listen to:

■ *Beware your credit cards.* Delay the gratification on purchases if you can't immediately afford them. Young people rack up insane amounts of debt for no good reason, and Jack should avoid bad debts.

■ *Contribute to your company's 401(k).* Starting early does a couple of great things. First, it gives Jack's savings a very long time to compound. Small amounts invested now lead to big gains later. Second, it starts good habits. And heck, since it's money that's withheld from his salary, he's never going to miss it anyway!

FLOWERING FRANK AND FIONA

NAME: Frank and Fiona Fawkes

AGES: Frank 29; Fiona 27

CAREER STAGES: Frank has got his first major promotion; Fiona teaches in a private school

MARITAL STATUS: Married ten months

CHILDREN: None, yet

LIVING SITUATION: Apartment, but looking to move

SALARY: Combined $73,000

CURRENT RETIREMENT SAVINGS: $17,000

MAJOR OBLIGATIONS: $34,000 student loans; $7,000 car loan; $5,000 credit card debt

MAJOR UPCOMING EXPENSES: House down payment

Frank and Fiona are getting ready to start a family life—kids, the house, et cetera, et cetera. But the truth is, they've got their work cut out for them. They have some credit card debt that crept into their lives in the run-up to their wedding. Plus, they need to have about $30,000 in cash to buy a house in the neighborhood where they want to live. They're eager to buy, and they've discussed removing money from their work retirement plans so that they can buy into that house sooner than later, perhaps a lot later.

The thought of retirement savings doesn't seem very relevant to these two right now, what with all the demands on their money.

I have some suggestions for the Fawkes family:

- *Understand that patience may very well be a great virtue.* I sympathize completely with the desire to own a home; however, rushing into a purchase now could be seriously counterproductive, as the following bullet points will show.

- *The credit cards need to be paid off.* Don't even *think* about putting money aside for a down payment until those balances are at zero. Fuggedaboutit!

- *Leave the retirement plans alone.* Really. The credit card debt should be manageable in a short period of time without any extreme sacrifice, so you don't need the 401(k) money for that. Withdrawing from the 401(k) for the sake of getting the money for the house is a serious (and all too common) mistake. There are serious penalties and tax ramifications for taking money out of a 401(k) early. Plus, the money removed from the account wouldn't be compounding. Following through on this withdrawal would be a very bad idea. (Note that some 401(k) providers allow borrowing against a retirement plan, but strict rules for repayment apply. Research thoroughly before you consider this.)

- *Set up a very tight budget.* With such ambitious near-term plans, they need to get a handle on where every dollar goes so they can determine exactly how much they can save. With some discipline and some patience, things should come together before too long.

YURI, EUNICE, AND YOUNGSTERS

NAME: Yuri and Eunice Urstead

AGES: Yuri 42; Eunice 39

CAREER STAGES: Yuri works part-time as a graphic designer; Eunice, an engineer, is a manager at a small firm.

MARITAL STATUS: Married eleven years

CHILDREN: Three; ages 2, 6, 9

LIVING SITUATION: Three-bedroom house

SALARY: Combined $121,000

CURRENT RETIREMENT SAVINGS: $95,000

MAJOR OBLIGATIONS: Mortgage, all kinds of expenses with the kids, two nice cars

MAJOR UPCOMING EXPENSES: Family vacation to Disney World; deeply concerned about college costs

Yuri and Eunice can't quite figure out how, with an income of over $100,000 per year, things are so tight. They don't think they're living lavishly: Their house is nice but not gaudy; their cars aren't extravagant either. But that's their life now, and they're seeing some difficult times on the horizon. For starters, though they're making ends meet, Eunice is concerned about her company's long-term viability. And they have almost no idea of how they're going to pay the tuition for three children.

In this mess of finances, they haven't spent much time thinking about retirement. They know that they really should, and they know that their current savings are inadequate, but they don't know how to balance the current pressures with those future needs. Eunice continues to make a 5 percent contribution to her 401(k), but that's all they're doing.

My suggestions for Yuri and Eunice:

■ *Come to terms with the idea that $100,000 isn't what it used to be.* You can live comfortably, but in some major metropolitan areas that sum doesn't afford nearly as much as you might think it should. (New Yorkers know this all too well!)

■ *Eliminate extravagances.* Yuri and Eunice need to do some forensics on their finances. For a three-month period they should be tracking their expenses with extreme detail. When they do that, they're almost certain to find "leaks," places where they're spending far more than they imagined. Maybe they're spending too much on clothes, maybe their food budget is too high. Only they can do the research that will get them the answers they need.

- *Prioritize an emergency fund.* They've got almost nothing in reserves, and with Eunice's company being unstable, they really need to have some cash to fall back on should the company fold or downsize Eunice out of a job. They should have at least three months' expenses in emergency reserves.

- *Take a very close look at insurance.* With Eunice earning the vast majority of the family's income, the family needs to be sure that Eunice is adequately insured. What life insurance comes with her job? What disability? Would it be enough, or anywhere near, should something happen to her. Without proper insurance, if something were to happen to Eunice, her family's lifestyle could absolutely collapse. (Note: I'm not an insurance expert. Do some research to see that you're properly insured.)

- *Come to understand the realities of college expenses.* The family's youngest will start college in nine years if all goes well. The estimates of what a four-year private college costs at that time are just staggering. Their oldest could easily spend over $200,000 on tuition and living costs. And the fact of the matter is that while Yuri and Eunice could contribute to a child's education, it looks like there's no way, short of some lottery score, that they'll be able to afford the costs for three kids.

- *Emphasize retirement.* If Yuri and Eunice want to do their kids a favor, they'll get serious about their retirement savings. Sure, having some money for college expenses would be great, but they don't have it, and they're not going to have it. At this rate, there's a chance that they could become serious burdens on their kids later in life. No one wants to be dependent on children; it would be humiliating for everyone involved. But if Yuri and Eunice run out of money, some really bad situations could arise. They need to start maxing out every tax-preferred account that's available to them—starting with their 401(k)s and IRAs.

PLUS-FIFTY PAUL AND PATRICIA

NAME: Paul and Patricia Patrick
AGES: Paul 52; Patricia 52
CAREER STAGES: Paul is an editor at a small publisher; Patricia is a free-lance writer
MARITAL STATUS: Married twenty-seven years
CHILDREN: Two; ages 24, 22
LIVING SITUATION: Three-bedroom house
SALARY: Combined $84,000
CURRENT RETIREMENT SAVINGS: $168,000
MAJOR OBLIGATIONS: Retirement
MAJOR UPCOMING EXPENSES: Daughter's wedding

Paul and Patricia are getting to the point where retirement is on the horizon. They both have projects in mind for their retirement and are looking forward to the long stretches of time that will allow them to pursue their passions. Paul has grown frustrated at his job, where the company's change of direction in recent years conflicts with his own vision and purpose. He'd like to get out sooner rather than later. Patricia, who writes for a variety of magazines and newspapers, now finds the hustle that's needed to land work as a freelancer a little exhausting.

They are becoming aware that they have not put nearly enough time and energy into their retirement planning. The amount that they currently have in retirement accounts seems far too small.

The Patricks need to make some changes, and the sooner they embrace this reality, the better.

■ *Get serious about your financial education.* These are people who never enjoyed talk of finance. I understand that, I never did either.

But now they, and I, need to be more attentive. We need to make a conscious decision that this *is* a priority.

■ *Look seriously at projections.* They should look at a variety of on-line retirement calculators to get a full understanding of the situation they're currently in. These calculators will let them play with a number of variables, including their desired retirement income, retirement age, and the rate of return on their investments. It will give them a good idea of the sorts of changes they can make to get their retirement planning on track.

■ *Start implementing the changes.* The Patricks, quite frankly, have a limited number of options. Of course, they need to save as much as they possibly can, maxing out 401(k)s and IRAs. They should look for any other savings they can find, but, frankly, it's unlikely that scrimping here and there is going to lead them to a comfortable retirement. These folks need to make some fundamental changes. In the broadest view, these sorts of changes fit into two categories:

— *They can change their plans* and decide to work longer before retiring.

— *They can downsize sooner rather than later.* The Patricks had planned on downsizing to a condo at some point, maybe a small two-bedroom, during retirement. But doing that now may be the best way for them to ensure that they can sock away money on a weekly and monthly basis. In the end, the Patricks may not love the move, but life may be a bit more comfortable. They won't have to live the rest of their lives on an austerity budget.

PROFITING PETER AND STEPHANIE

NAME: Peter and Stephanie Stefanson
AGES: Peter 49; Stephanie 42
CAREER STAGES: Peter is a financial planner for celebrities; Stephanie is a stay-at-home mom

MARITAL/STATUS: Married for fifteen years

CHILDREN: Two; ages 12, 10

LIVING SITUATION: New York City, four-bedroom duplex on the Upper West Side

SALARY: $500,000+

CURRENT RETIREMENT SAVINGS: $225,000

MAJOR OBLIGATIONS: Mortgage, lavish lifestyle, private school for kids, vacations up the wazoo, nice clothing, and a Ferrari

MAJOR UPCOMING EXPENSES: Triple bypass surgery for Peter due to stressful job; vacation; time off from work

Now, you may think that because Peter is a very successful businessman, with a seemingly secure job he and Stephanie wouldn't have to worry about money at all. Ah, but here's the rub: Wealth, like most everything else in life, is relative. If you make very little money, but your expenses are very small; well, then, you certainly wouldn't be living as "large" as Peter and Stephanie, but because Peter and Stephanie have set themselves up with such a lavish lifestyle, they need a lot more to get by. Their monthly nut is so large that if Peter's surgery requires him to take a lot of time off, or even worse, perhaps to retire due to the stress of his job, then he may be in just as bad shape as someone with a much lower income, in terms of his ability to support his family's lifestyle. And he may be totally screwed if he's forced to retire early.

You'd be surprised at how many high income and high net worth families are ill prepared for retirement. In order for them to continue to live in the luxury they are accustomed to, they have to plan just as well—if not better—then most others. If you make $500,000 a year but your expenses are $400,000, then you aren't saving all that much relative to your lifestyle, and if you have a disaster in terms of not being able to work, then even if you have a nice pot of gold saved up, it won't last you very long unless you're willing and able to change your family's lifestyle.

You'd be even more surprised at how many people of high net worth don't think they even need an IRA, or much of one, feeling that they will always have more than enough, so they neglect the one thing that will potentially allow them to continue to live the life they've designed.

So, for them, as for everyone else, *planning*—strict, diligent planning—is paramount if they're going to have a pleasurable retirement. They need to look carefully at the risks they're inviting. Remember that Peter basically works for himself, so if surgery keeps him sidelined for long, his clients will probably have to find someone else to help them with their finances. He could quickly find himself without much of any income at all.

We hear about celebrities and rich power couples filing for bankruptcy all the time. Wayne Newton, Mike Tyson, Elton John, Burt Reynolds, and dozens more have all had their share of overspending. Once again, you'll hear me say, "I can relate!" If you can relate, which many of you can, I am sure, then rather than being frustrated, now is the time to take control of the situation, now is the time to Rule Your Freakin' Retirement! Okay, there, I said it. I said it and I feel good about it!

I remember reading about Roberto Duran, the great boxer who had earned something like $20 million in his career and found himself broke and struggling to make ends meet. As the New York Knicks star center Patrick Ewing once said while negotiating for a better contract for the NBA player's union, "We might make a lot of money, but we also spend a lot of money."

The more you have, the more you can spend, but if your income takes a pause, you can eat up your savings and your retirement pretty fast. Take it from me, again. I have done this several times and it hurts when you have to regroup, change your lifestyle, and start from scratch. That's why the best thing to do is follow the same rules as anyone else, no matter how much money you have.

As far as Peter's IRA goes, he can afford to be more invested in the stock market because he can afford more risk exposure, but I still would not recommend being too heavily invested. You know me, I don't trust the stock market to just continue to plow higher and no one wants to see his 401(k) become the dreaded 201K.

WAXIE'S NOTE

I think the stock market is headed lower, a lot lower!

Conclusion

Whatever your situation, you should find some common ground within these examples if you look hard enough. No one's situation is exactly the same as anyone else's, but there are some commonalities. The point is that your situation and your needs and desires need to be respected and planned for. In order to Rule Your Freakin' Retirement, you'll need to map out a real solid plan and implement it. There's no time like the present, and the present is *now!*

Quiz

1. **Which of the following plans is MOST important for young single people to contribute to from day one of their working lives?**

   a. Term life insurance

   b. Company 401(k)

   c. Real estate holdings

   d. Roth IRA

   Answer: b

2. **Carefully breaking down a family's expenses over a three-month period is important in which of the following circumstances:**

   a. You're unaware of what your needs are in retirement

   b. You're unaware of what portion of your monthly income goes where

c. You're unsure if you'll be able to afford a looming expense

d. An exercise like this is a good idea for everyone

Answer: d

3. *What's an appropriate minimum amount to have in emergency reserves?*

a. 3 months expenses

b. 4 months expenses

c. 6 months expenses

d. 12 months expenses

Answer: a

4. *Put the following financial priorities in their correct order— that is, which should you accomplish before moving on to the next?*

a. Saving for a down payment for a home

b. 401(k)

c. Paying off credit card debt

d. Children's college fund

Answer: c, b, a, d

Chapter 4

Social Security and Your Retirement

Every few years a major politician gets it into his head that he's going to do something about the country's immense entitlement programs— Social Security and Medicare. The programs, we're told, can't continue as they are. No way, they shout from the rafters! They devour way too much of the federal budget, stripping the country of its wealth. There are even grave warnings about the sustainability of the programs: If something isn't done, they'll surely go broke. We've heard it from George W. Bush, with Karl Rove's assistance, Bill Clinton, and others. In the 2008 primary campaign season, every single candidate in the primaries (all seventeen of them*) had a position on Social Security reform. And every one of them was correct in their humble opinions.

Invariably, calls for change are met by cries of protest. Lobbying from interest groups gets fierce, and soon members of Congress are getting a firm message in their home districts: No cuts, no way. They

*Rudy Giuliani, John McCain, Mitt Romney, Sam Brownback, Mike Huckabee, Fred Thompson, Tom Tancredo, Ron Paul, Tommy Thompson, John Edwards, Hillary Clinton, Barack Obama, Bill Richardson, Dennis Kucinich, Joseph Biden, Christopher Dodd, Mike Gravel. Information obtained from the Cato Institute Web site: http://www.socialsecurity.org.

go back to Washington and dig in. They assure their constituents that nothing will happen with these programs, which so many hold so dear.

It's the kind of situation that makes me sympathetic to everyone involved—or most of them anyway. When Clinton and Bush and others decided to take on the entitlement programs, they were attempting a good thing. The programs *are* out of control. (We'll talk a little more about the troubling economics of Social Security soon.) Some serious changes to Social Security and Medicare are going to happen eventually. There's no way around it, and the sooner the better.

Yet I also understand why so many people—seniors in particular—get panicky when there's any talk of changes to these programs. People rely on these entitlements. For some, it's all they've got. Without Social Security and Medicare, they'd have nothing. Zero, zilch, nada—absolutely nothing. Of course, they bitch to their congressmen when the livelihoods they've been promised are threatened. And who can blame them. Not I, not I.

Given the turbulent present and potential changes to the country's entitlement programs, it's worth asking what form Social Security will take when those in their thirties and forties reach retirement age. Obviously, I can't answer this question. But for those in their fifties and sixties, it's unlikely that the program will change in any substantive way during their lifetime. I can't guarantee that, of course, but you are likely to get all the benefits that the government says you're due. The remainder of this chapter discusses the specifics of Social Security as it exists today and how we can expect it to be for some time.

How Social Security Works

Social Security is funded through FICA payments—that extremely nasty chunk of taxes removed from your paycheck. I don't know anyone who likes FICA payments. I don't care what party they are affiliated with. The money is put in the Social Security Trust Fund, where it's invested in government-backed securities. All Social Security payments—to retirees and to those who have suffered disabilities—come out of this fund.

The money you put into the Social Security Trust Fund is paid out to current retirees quickly. The money that you pay in does not, as some people think, go into an account that is specific to you. There's not some government equivalent of a bank where your FICA payments are stored and gaining interest, though that is an idea that has some political backing. Your contributions and mine from today's paychecks pay benefits to today's retirees. The thought—the hope— is that the next generations of wage earners will be able to pay for us when we're into retirement.

The obvious and oft-discussed problem is that the demographics make this young-supports-the-old structure difficult to sustain. For one thing, people are living longer. As of 2005, the average life expectancy of Americans was 77.8 years. For those making it to retirement age, the life expectancy is even longer. So people are spending more time on Social Security then they used to. The other issue is that people are having fewer children. The baby-boom generation is huge when compared with the Gen X, Gen Y, and Gen Next. Within a few years, there are going to be a lot of people to support. According to the Social Security Administration, the changing demographics will exhaust the Social Security Trust Fund by 2041 if changes aren't made. At that point, revenues generated by FICA will cover only about 75 percent of Social Security's obligations. These numbers change as forecasts change, so the outlook may be slightly more optimistic or pessimistic by the time you read this book. And, of course, it all depend on what other crisis (isn't there always one?) money needs to be diverted to.

Social Security's original intent was to help the lower-income folks in our society get by in their retirement. People of lesser income will receive a greater of proportion of their incomes from Social Security than those who are wealthier. In fact, some people think that people of really high income shouldn't receive any money from the Social Security system. That's why from time to time someone brings up the idea of means testing Social Security, which would determine who could get any benefits at all. Means testing hasn't found much support in the halls of Congress. I'll leave it to you to figure out why. It ain't tough.

Paying In, Getting Money Out

In order to receive Social Security benefits when you retire, you have to have made contributions during your working life. To qualify, you have to have enough credits. In 2007, every $1,000 in income you receive nets you one credit. You can attain a maximum of four credits a year, one for each quarter you work. You will only receive Social Security if you accumulate forty credits through your work life. If you work a full ten years throughout your life, you'll be eligible.

Exactly how much you'll be getting from Social Security will depend on a few factors—how much you've earned primarily, but when you decide to take your benefits and your spouse's situation enter into the calculation. You'll need to do some thinking and figuring to give yourself the best chance of getting the most money out of the system.

Keep in mind as you read this chapter that the rules may very well change at some point before you retire. In fact, unless you're retiring imminently I can almost guarantee it'll go through a change or two. Changes in Social Security law could very well affect your budget. So keep your ears open when Social Security is talked about on the nightly news; it could be very important to your life.

Full Retirement Age

Every year the Social Security Administration sends you a sheet that tells you how much you can expect to get in retirement. The sheet gives figures for several ages at which you might claim benefits. Depending on your age, you might see figures for ages 62 through 67. The key number to look at is what Social Security calls your full retirement age, which is, quite simply, the point at which you'd receive 100 percent of the benefits you're entitled to. For a long, long time, the full retirement age was 65; but to ease some demands on the Social Security system, the full retirement age was raised to 67 for those born after 1959. Look at Table 4-1 to find your full retirement age.

TABLE 4-1. FULL RETIREMENT AGE FOR YEAR OF BIRTH

YEAR OF BIRTH	FULL RETIREMENT AGE
1937 or earlier	65
1938	65 + 2 months
1939	65 + 4 months
1940	65 + 6 months
1941	65 + 8 months
1942	65 + 10 months
1943–1954	66
1955	66 + 2 months
1956	66 + 4 months
1957	66 + 6 months
1958	66 + 8 months
1959	66 + 10 months
1960 and after	67

If you decide to retire before your full retirement age, you will only receive a percentage of your full amount. The exact reduction from your full benefit depends on your year of birth and the age at which you choose to retire. Table 4-2 shows some of the reductions in benefits you could expect from early retirement.

TABLE 4-2. PERCENTAGE OF BENEFITS RECEIVED WHEN CLAIMING PRIOR TO FULL RETIREMENT AGE

YEAR OF BIRTH	AGE OF RETIREMENT	PERCENTAGE OF FULL BENEFIT RECEIVED
1937 or earlier	62	80.0
1937 or earlier	64	93.3
1943–1954	62	75.0
1943–1954	65	93.3
1957	62	72.5
1957	65	90.0
1960 or later	62	70.0
1960 or later	65	86.7

See the tables at http://www.ssa.gov/retire2/agereduction.htm to see all the percentage reductions associated with your year of birth. If you happen to be in the fortunate place where you can put off applying for benefits beyond your full retirement age, you can get more money still. Social Security offers what it calls delayed retirement credits. For every month or year you put off collecting benefits beyond your full retirement age, your monthly check will increase by a specified percentage. Table 4-3 shows the effect of delayed retirement on your benefits.

The benefit increase ceases at age 70, so there's no point in not collecting your Social Security benefits at that time. Frankly, if it's there when you are eligible, as they used to say when I was a kid looking to cash out from the local bookie: Take da money and run! Fast as lightning.

TABLE 4-3. BENEFITS ASSOCIATED WITH DELAYING RETIREMENT PAST FULL RETIREMENT AGE

YEAR OF BIRTH	YEARLY RATE OF INCREASE	MONTHLY RATE OF INCREASE
1933–1934	5.5%	11/24 of 1%
1935–1936	6.0%	1/2 of 1%
1937–1938	6.5%	13/24 of 1%
1939–1940	7.0%	7/12 of 1%
1941–1942	7.5%	5/8 of 1%
1943 or later	8.0%	2/3 of 1%

Spousal Benefits

Social Security has a number of rules when it comes to providing a married or divorced couple with benefits. You may be surprised to learn that a spouse who has never worked is still entitled to up to 50 percent of the benefits offered to the working member of the family. So if the husband was the sole earner of the household and was getting $1,000 a month in Social Security, the wife could be eligible for up to $500 more.

The 50 percent for the nonworking spouse will only be available if the main earner puts off a claim to benefits until the full retirement age. If the main breadwinner claims benefits before that time, the checks will be smaller. The exact amounts will be determined by the age at which the claim is made and the birth year of the spouse. For example, if a spouse born in 1955 claimed benefits at age 62, he or she would be eligible for 34 percent of the earning spouse's benefit. At age 65 he or she would be eligible for 45.1 percent. At age 66 and 2 months, which is full retirement age, he or she would be eligible for a full 50 percent. The best way to find out exactly what percentage of the primary earner's check a spouse would receive is to check the tables at the Social Security Web site: http://www.ssa.gov/retire2/agereduction.htm.

Note that if one member of a married couple earns a small income, the spouse is entitled to either the benefits he or she would have earned independently or the amount due a nonworking spouse, whichever is greater.

Working After Collecting Social Security

Some people consider collecting Social Security benefits while still part of the workforce. You can do this, but you need to be aware that under certain conditions you won't receive all the benefit you might have been expecting. Should you continue working beyond your full retirement age, you don't need to worry about any deductions from your Social Security check. That wouldn't make sense at all. However, if you're under the full retirement age, there is a limit to what you can make without seeing a deduction. In 2007, that limit was $12,960. This number changes every year and is determined by a mathematical formula tied to annual wages. Check the Social Security Web site for the current exempt amount if you're nearing retirement.

For everything you make over the limit, Social Security will deduct one dollar from your benefits for every dollar you earn. If you do work and earn more than the exempt amount, Social Security will give you credit for the additional work and your benefit will be re-calculated accordingly. You'll see an increase in your benefit once you do fully retire.

When to Take Social Security

When you get into your sixties, you'll have to make a pretty big decision. Do you take your Social Security benefits early, or do you hold off for a while, to your full retirement age or beyond. According to the Social Security Administration most people opt to get their benefits early. Many of these people have no choice; they absolutely need that money to live. But getting your benefits as early as possible may not be the best plan for you.

Viewed retirementally, you have a single goal: to get as many dollars from Social Security as you possibly can. The question, then, is whether you'll make more by taking benefits earlier or later.

The calculation is pretty simple. Say you were born in 1954, so your full retirement age is 66. At that time you'd be entitled to $12,000 per year. You look at the tables at http://www.ssa.gov/retire2/agereduction.htm and find that if you retire at age 62, you'll be entitled to 75 percent of that amount, or $9,000. In the four years between the minimum age and the full retirement age, you'll take in $36,000. So the question becomes: How long will it take you to recoup that $36,000? By waiting to age 66, you'll get an extra $3,000 a year so it would take twelve years, till age 78, for the numbers to even out. (Note that all of these calculations ignore inflation and use stationary dollar values; actual Social Security benefits are adjusted for inflation.)

This simple calculation overlooks the investment income you'll gain by taking your Social Security benefits early. The money that you take from Social Security is money that you won't need to take from your IRAs and other retirement accounts that are generating returns. The exact amount of the extra savings depends on the return you'd be expecting from your investments. Generally, you can figure another couple of years to recoup investment income.

For most people, the break-even will be right around age 80 or 81. There are a variety of online calculators you can use to get a more precise calculation.

Whatever your break-even age is, you're going to need to make some judgment as to whether or not you'll live that long. You may be uncomfortable making this calculation, but you need to look at your health and your family history and make the best bet that you can. If you think you have a relatively short life ahead of you, take the money early; if not, wait—if you can. Given that most people who make it to retirement age have pretty long life spans, your best bet usually is to wait.

Once you've got a decent idea of what you'll be getting from Social Security, you can factor it into the retirement budget we talked about in chapter 3.

Quiz

1. **How many quarters must you work in your life before you qualify for Social Security?**

   a. 7

   b. 8

   c. 9

   d. 10

   Answer: d

2. **What is the full retirement age for someone born in 1965?**

   a. 62

   b. 64

   c. 65

   d. 67

   Answer: d

3. **What percentage of full benefits would a person receive if that person was born in 1954 and retired at age 65?**

   a. 78

   b. 86

   c. 93

   d. 96

   Answer: c

4. **At what age do delayed retirement credits cease?**

   a. 69

   b. 70

   c. 71

   d. 72

   Answer: d

5. **True or false: A nonworking spouse is entitled to Social Security benefits.**

   a. True

   b. False

   Answer a

6. **For most retirees, the breakeven usually comes at what age?**

   a. 65

   b. 70

   c. 75

   d. 80

   e. 85

   Answer: b

Chapter 5

Saving for College

Working families today face a huge challenge when it comes to saving for college. The ballooning costs are astonishing. A family with two kids could incur more than a quarter of a million dollars on bachelor's degrees alone if both kids go to private schools. Trust me, having two beautiful girls and living in New York City ain't cheap. And what if one of the kids wants a master's in art history?! How can you possibly afford it? Most of us are going to feel the pinch of those expenses at some point.

Yet before you ask about the "how," you need to back up and ask an even simpler question: *Should* I fund my kid's education?

This is a tough question. And it's one you need to approach soberly and honestly. Don't let emotion—your heartfelt desire to provide for this stage of your kid's development—rule your head. It may sound cold-blooded and hard-hearted, but if you don't make the best decision for the best reasons, you could do yourself and your kids more harm than good in the long run.

Here are some of the major factors to consider when considering whether or not you should save for your kid's higher education costs:

- *Will saving for college come at the expense of crucial retirement savings?* We've spent a good deal of time considering the amounts of money that will be needed in retirement, and the amounts of savings it will take to get there. You developed some sort of plan that includes hard numbers—the amount you have and the amount you'll need to save—so that you can retire comfortably. If saving for college endangers this plan in any way, *don't do it.* It's far more important for your children that you be prepared to support yourself in your later years than that their tuition is taken care of. As I tell my trendfund.com clients, it's a marathon, not a sprint. You want your kids to be taken care of? Take care of yourself first! There's usually some combination of grants and loans and scholarships that will allow a kid to attend the college of his choice. He or she may have a ton of debt by the time he or she graduates, and that's unfortunate, but it may be necessary. The rates on student loans aren't too bad. Repayment of the loans may be a drag, but for most students, it's manageable. So, in all likelihood, your child will be able to go to the school of his or her choice (or perhaps a decent state school alternative) whether you save for it or not. Now think about the consequences that could befall your child if you fail to save adequately for retirement. You could be forced to move in with your grown child's family because you can't afford to live on your own. That's no good for anyone.

■ *Are college savings eating into your tax advantages?* This point is related to the previous one. Even if you feel you have about enough saved for retirement and you wish to fund an educational account, you should think long and hard about such a decision. Money that doesn't go to the government is money that stays in the family. The best way to keep money out of Uncle Sam's pocket is to make the maximum contribution to your 401(k)s and IRAs. If you're not making the most of these tax savings, you're probably making a mistake. (Note: There are college savings plans with some tax advantages. These 529 plans, which I'll discuss in detail later, are okay, but they won't give you nearly the savings you'll get out of a 401(k).)

- *Will saving this way be a problem when it comes time to apply for financial aid?* When colleges determine what sorts of financial aid are available to students, they make some complex calculations to determine a family's wealth. Bank accounts, brokerage accounts, and 529 accounts are included in the family's assets. Retirement accounts, however, are not included as a family asset. So getting as much money as you possibly can in your retirement accounts could lead to a big cost savings when financial aid is calculated.

The theme here should be pretty clear: retirement planning first, college later *if* it's possible.

529 Plans

Those who have saved enough for retirement and wish to start a fund for their children's education can get acquainted with yet another type of account named for a section of the tax code—529s. Section 529 gave the states (and the District of Columbia) the right to set up educational savings plans that have some decent tax advantages. The specifics of the plan are largely left to the states, and not surprisingly, implementations vary widely from state to state. Some offer tax advantages; some offer close to nothing and are probably best avoided.

The states' 529 plans fall into two major categories: prepaid tuition programs and college savings plans.

WAXIE'S TIP: Gifting

One of the great advantages of 529 programs is that they provide an excellent way for grandparents and other relatives to contribute large amounts to a child's education without paying gift taxes. As of 2006, a single person could contribute up to $60,000 in a single year without incurring gift taxes. This amount will be prorated over five years.

Prepaid Tuition Programs

A prepaid tuition program locks in the price of tuition. You pay a lump sum today, or stretch out monthly payments over a period of time, and thereby guarantee that your child's full tuition is covered. Usually, the state offering the prepaid plan will tie the price to the current rate charged at state universities. When it comes time for the child to go to college, he or she can go to a state school knowing that the full tuition is covered. Or if the child chooses to go out of state or to a private school, the prepaid plan will pay a portion of the tuition that is equivalent to what is charged at the state schools.

These plans have a couple of key advantages:

■ *They avoid steep rises in college costs.* The costs of attending colleges have been skyrocketing, far outpacing the rate of inflation or the return on most common investments. Locking in the price of tuition with a prepaid plan protects you from future increases.

■ *They are a guaranteed investment.* Often (but not always) prepaid tuition programs are guaranteed by the state sponsoring the program. You won't have to worry about market forces playing with your kid's college fund as you would if the money were put into mutual funds.

Illinois offers a good example of a prepaid 529 plan. Say you live in Illinois and want to cover four years (eight semesters) of tuition for your kindergarten-age kid at a state school. In 2006, you could pay $43,773 in a lump sum, $885 per month for five years, or $531 per month for ten years to cover the full tuition. You could also choose from plans that cover fewer semesters or one that mixes a down payment and monthly benefits.

Contributions to prepaid plans may offer relief from state taxes. In Illinois, for example, up to $20,000 in 529 contributions will not be counted as income for state tax purposes for couples filing jointly.

College Savings Plan

Unlike prepaid plans, 529 college savings plans don't offer any guarantees. Instead, your contributions are put in the hands of an investment house, like TIAA-CREF, Fidelity, or Vanguard. The money is then put in a mix of funds. Depending on the plan, you may or may not have some control over the investment products. The New York 529 is managed by Vanguard and contributors to the plan can choose from fifteen plans that have different allocations. Some allocations are labeled "aggressive," others "moderately aggressive," and some are more "conservative."

The hope is that, over time, the investments will gain in value and will help offset some college costs. Just remember, hope is a "killer"; it's a passive way to go about things. This is our freakin' retirement, babies; our job is to be totally prepared, ironclad, so whatever investing you do, make sure it's as ironclad as possible.

Some 529 college savings plans offer decent tax benefits. With the New York State plan, for example, up to $10,000 can be deducted from state taxes by couples filing jointly. In addition, any gains seen within the plan will be free of federal and state taxes. Then, when it comes time to withdraw money for tuition and other higher education expenses, the money taken from the 529 will not be taxed on either the federal or state level.

If you're considering a college savings plan, you really need to look into the specific benefits offered by your state. In California, for example, initial contributions receive no favorable tax treatment. Without this advantage, it may not be worth contributing to the California plan at all. You may very well do better to have the money in a brokerage account, where you can trade in and out of any stock or fund that suits your fancy. You also avoid the management fee that is charged by the company administering the funds, which can be as high as 0.5 percent.

WAXIE'S TIP: Penalties

These programs were created for saving for college. If you withdraw the funds for any reasons other than qualified educational expenses, you'll be hit with income taxes on the withdrawal, plus a 10 percent penalty. In trading parlance (at least at trendfund.com) we call that a *big ka-chingo!* As opposed to what we want, lots of ka-chingos!

Quiz

1. *True or false: Most 529 plans have tax advantages that are equal to those of a 401(k).*

   a. True

   b. False

   Answer: b

2. *True or false: All 529 plans offer a guaranteed rate of return.*

   a. True

   b. False

   Answer: b

3. *The process through which family members can contribute large sums to 529 plans while avoiding most taxes is known by what name?*

   a. Family College Assistance Program

   b. Send a Kid to School Program

   c. Keep It in the Family

   d. Gifting

   Answer: d

4. *True or false: Funds placed in a 529 account can be withdrawn at any time without penalty.*

   a. True

   b. False

   Answer: b

Chapter 6

Real Estate

Okay, let's deal with a topic that is pretty sensitive as I write this, and chances are it'll still be sensitive when you start reading this. I'm writing this chapter in mid-2008. I wanted to wait as long as possible before I addressed real estate and its role in retirement, because as you no doubt know, the real estate market throughout the country is in a state of crisis. Some smart people feel that this is the worst period for real estate in the history of the country. Every day I open the paper, there's more bad news on the real estate front—foreclosures are growing at an alarming rate, home prices are diving in many parts of the country, with parts of California and the Midwest being absolutely slaughtered. If the real estate market were a tree it would surely be chopped down and used as firewood. In fact, many homes might be worth more as firewood, unfortunately. Trust me, I don't make light of it, other than for the strong belief that humor is sometimes the only way to deal with tragedy. And there really is no other way to look at the real estate market, at least as I write this, than tragic.

There are myriad reasons for this scary state of affairs. Most have been well documented and I don't want to go into too much detail here, but there are a few causes I want to touch on. Too many people were loaned *waaaay* too much money. Banks offered adjustable rate mortgages (ARMs) to people with little means—folks who could barely afford to make their first payments. The interest rates shot up after a defined initial period of low interest, and the monthly payments went way, way up. Suddenly a barely affordable house became completely beyond their means. Prices fell as houses flooded the market and soon there was no way of selling anything. Buyers couldn't sell and had little choice but to let the banks foreclose on their most prized possession. For many, the American dream has been devastated. I feel for all those affected.

Another major factor in the real estate market's downward spiral was extensive speculation. In the decade previous to the crisis, real estate values exploded. Everyone wanted a piece of the wealth that was being generated. Everyone was in the real estate biz. Cable television was filled with shows dedicated to house flipping—*Flip This House, Flip That House,* were just two of the catchy titles. People bought houses and condos that they never intended to live in. "We'll flip it. Make a killing." You have no idea how many clients of mine at trendfund.com e-mailed me or took me aside at seminars and told me they had a great real estate deal for me to invest in. How do you know you're at a top in any market? When everyone is a self-proclaimed expert on how to make money in it!

I spent some time in Vegas, where the market is in horrible shape. The strip is lined now with luxury high-rise condos that are almost entirely unoccupied. At the end of 2008 there will be roughly 15,000 condos on the market for sale. Many of these were bought by speculators, those who thought they could gobble one of these units up and turn it over without ever living in it. Now the buildings are almost entirely dark, and many buyers are absolutely desperate to unload their properties at any price. But no one is buying. The same is apparent in New York City, where I live, and where I heard for years how New York was impervious to a real estate market downturn, because, well, because it's New York. Darn it! *WRONG!* When a market bursts, very rarely does it pop in only a few places, it pops *everywhere.* So much construction, not enough people who have $2 to $5 *million* for a three- or four-bedroom apartment. Values have to plummet. It's a pretty simple equation if ya think about it! Simple, and simply painful.

I'm not a real estate expert, and I've never claimed to be. But I do understand a thing or two about how markets work. And with this knowledge, I would have cautioned anyone against speculating like these people did, or for that matter, spending more on a house than they could reasonably afford.

Why? When you get to part III of this book, where I get into my true expertise, trend trading, you'll see that I constantly warn against putting too much money on any single trade or position. I know with absolute certainty that many of the trades I enter into are going to lose me money. Markets *are* unpredictable, and sometimes I'll get it wrong. But I'm successful because I'm often right, and I know how to get out of bad trade when it doesn't work. I *never, absolutely never,* have so much riding on a single trade that the outcome could seriously hurt my financial stability.

In the real estate market of the previous years, tens of thousands of people made this exact error: They made a single investment that could seriously kick their ass if it went south. They didn't understand that any investment, especially short-term ones, come with a degree of risk. Sure, the housing market had been strong for a very long time, but that was no guarantee of indefinite growth. A lot of people just didn't get it.

Will real estate be a viable investment in the near future? In some places, sure. On a broad scale things may recover. But I really don't know what the future holds in the real estate world. This unpredictability puts some of the most basic financial planning rules into question. For example, just about every financial advisor says that the most important thing you can do is get out of renting and buy something. The argument is that you're gaining equity in your house, whereas with rent, you're just seeing that money disappear. In addition to the equity, your home will gain value over time. That's the prevailing wisdom being: real estate *always* goes up in the end! Phooey on that logic, folks, phooey! A market or a home value only goes up until it doesn't anymore. At some point there is a point where a market cannot possibly sustain itself any longer. It might eventually go higher, but it could take years, if not decades before doing so.

I read a variety of sources that said it was wise to buy if you thought you'd be in the house for three years. Some of these people I respect; they offered charts and graphs to bolster their contention that three years was enough of an horizon. Well, as it turned out in most places, if you bought in 2005, 2008 was a heck of a year to try and sell. In many parts of the country, you couldn't get near what you paid for your place, and that's not including broker's fees and other costs associated with selling.

To my mind, there's an open question as to how well real estate prices will rebound, and even if they do, I find it pretty hard to believe that real estate will see the same sort of gains that it has over the previous decades. We could very well be in for a long time of very stagnant housing prices.

If housing prices stay low and inventory remains high, renting could very well be a better option.

With so much flux and unpredictability in the housing markets, it's tough to offer a whole lot of wisdom on how you should proceed in the market. The best I can do is give some tips that I'm sure are sound. It's going to be pretty general. But given the state of things, I'd rather be vague than wrong.

Love It and Live in It

I'll reiterate something I said at the start of this book: Your house is primarily the place where you live. It's where you'll spend your days, and it will yield important memories for you and your family. You'll never have this sort of emotional involvement with another investment. So, when you're looking for property, get something that you can love and afford. Buy a place you want to live in for a decade, not three years. That way, if you stay put and the value goes up, you'll feel great. If the value drops some, who cares, you got a great place.

Be Sober About the Need to Sell

A lot of people like to downsize as they approach retirement. A smaller house better suits an empty nest, and the cost of maintenance on a small house or a condo can be a good deal less than a large house. Another factor is taxes. Older couples without school-age kids don't need to pay the high property taxes that come with good school districts.

When you're retired, saving on taxes and upkeep is a really big deal. But many people grow so attached to their homes that they look for reasons to stay in them beyond the point where it makes any sense. There are many people who have seen the values of their homes dip and decided to hold off on selling till prices recover. I know several people who have made this choice. But I don't think it makes all that much sense. If you're selling with the thought of downsizing, than the real question should concern the differential between the house you're selling and the one you want to buy. This number may not have changed much in the housing slump that we're in. And even if it has changed some, you need to think about a couple of other factors. Are the prices likely to change in the next few years? If you're very optimistic, then by all means hang on. What about the costs? Are you really comfortable absorbing them for years longer?

What I'm saying is, if it's time to sell, then go ahead and do it. Think it through, and do what you need to.

This advice applies especially to anyone who's considering a *reverse mortgage*. A reverse mortgage is a sort of home equity loan. Essentially, the bank gives you money, either in a lump sum, a monthly payment, or a line of credit. In return, the bank gains equity in your house. You don't have to repay your loan until you move or die.

For almost everyone, reverse mortgages are really bad news. They're extremely expensive. The fees and interest are very high. It almost always makes better fiscal sense to just sell your home, take whatever equity you have coming, and downscale appropriately. I think the only appropriate time to consider a reverse mortgage is for someone who's destitute, or close to death, and isn't concerned about leaving any sort of estate to his or her heirs. Even in these cases, he or she should consider it only when leaving a long-lived-in house is too horrifying to consider.

The people who will try to sell you such a mortgage are not looking out for your best interest. Salesmen make a fortune on reverse mortgages, so please be wary. If, after reading this, you're still considering a reverse mortgage, head over to the AARP Web site at http://www.aarp.org, where you can start some research to make sure it really is a good choice for you. If I haven't said it yet, retirement, like most things in life, is a lot about personal choices. What works for me might not work for you, or may very well work better for you than for me. In the end there is nothing perfect; perfection is an illusion. We're all doing the best we can to live the best life we can, and that, in the end, is what this book is about. I want you all to have a retirement that truly is a retirement. Healthy, happy, and comfortable financially you will be prepared for all the twists and turns life tends to take. In the end, you just need to Rule Your Freakin' Retirement! And, of course, read the next chapter!

Quiz

1. *What lesson can we learn from real estate speculators?*

   a. Having a large portion of your net worth tied up in any single investment leads to too much risk

   b. Quality neighborhoods offer the best investment opportunities

   c. All markets recover in a timely fashion

   d. Real estate investment should be avoided for the next five years

   Answer: a

2. *When buying a house, how long should you plan on living in it if you want to have a sound financial investment?*

   a. 1 year

   b. 2 years

   c. 3 years

   d. 5 years

   e. 10 years

   Answer: The longer the period, the better. I think ten years (e) is a good thought.

3. *Which of the following is not a factor in the housing crisis?*

   a. Overbuilding

   b. Lending to unqualified buyers

   c. Speculating

   d. Shoddy construction

   Answer: d

4. *Reverse mortgages are viable for which of the following groups?*

   a. Those looking to refinance

   b. Those looking for home equity loans for renovations

   c. Those with little income who are looking to stay in their homes

   d. Those who are considering buying additional properties

   Answer: c

Chapter 7

Insurance

When we're talking about anything in the realm of personal finance—whether it's saving properly for a home, deciding on investments, or coming up with a logical retirement plan—we tend to wear those rose-colored glasses people talk about all time. Know what I mean? When I talk about mutual funds and property and trend trading, and show how those can be used to make for a secure retirement, there's this big old assumption that I've made. I'm pretty sure you're making it yourself.

The assumption: You'll live till retirement and be in pretty good health in your preretirement and retirement years. But if you want to be really prepared—and be good to your family—you need to spend a little time thinking about some grim possibilities. The dreaded what-ifs.

I'll admit that I haven't been great in this area. When things are good in life, it's easy to look around and say, "Hey, I'm feeling good, looking good—(okay, maybe I could lose a couple of pounds)—but I'm healthy. My kids are beautiful. I'm thriving professionally. Knock on wood." You take in and admire your bounty, your luck. In these moments, who wants to stop and think about all that could go wrong?

Until recently, I hadn't spent much time thinking about potentially bad things. Until I woke up with a searing pain in my chest. I won't go into the details of the agony, my fright, or the terrifying visit to the hospital that followed. Suffice it to say that it wasn't a heart attack. It was my heart doing something it shouldn't have done and that I don't quite understand. It shook me up pretty good. And, yeah, I had a sorta "white light" type experience. Sounds hokey, but I did indeed see my life pass before my eyes, and in fact flatlined for a short period. (There's no such thing as short when you are talking about flatlining; death is pretty long-term, depending on your belief system, I guess.)

I was lucky. In a few weeks I was pretty much good as new. Well, almost. It's kinda like when I was a teenager and lived on the streets, homeless: You never forget. There's this scar that you have that allows a tiny little voice in the back of your brain to tell ya, "You're gonna suffer. Just grin and bear it!" Even today, when I get the flu, it sometimes feels like my heart is gonna burst. It ain't pretty, but like the little voice, it gets lesser and lesser and has less and less power as time does indeed heal *most* wounds!

In that short but horrible time, I thought about one thing and one thing only—my gorgeous, amazing daughter (my youngest daughter wasn't born yet). Most of what went through my head is tear-jerking and not germane to this book. So I'll spare you. However, there was one thing that entered my mind that is very much related to what you're reading about. While dealing with the terror and the pain, I started going through some math and paperwork. I was going through my memory, doing my best to recall whether all my paperwork was in order and organized. I was trying to identify any omissions in the care I planned for my daughter. At least that was part of it. It is amazing how much information can go through your mind in a matter of moments when you think you might not have much time left.

That, my friends, is what insurance is about. It's about putting aside the lazy, immature notion that things are fine and are certain to remain that way. It's about seeing that things will be okay for those we love when something horrible happens. We all know it can happen, but for the sake of hammering it through our thick skulls, I'll be extremely explicit: Terrible things happen, and they happen with an ugly regularity; 1.4 million people will get some form of cancer over the next year, according to the American Cancer Society. Each year, 30,000 Americans get into their cars and die before reaching their destinations. If you happen to be a coyote (ya know, the Wile E. sort), your chances of being hit by a falling anvil are almost 100 percent!

That's the point of this long preamble to the chapter. Bad stuff happens, and something may very well happen to you. That's why we have insurance. Because when things go bad, they can go really bad and the consequences can be horrific. Wile E. Coyote functions pretty well after getting nailed by an anvil. But you probably won't. An unforeseen event could leave you unable to work or dead. If you're being responsible to your family, you need to ensure that such an eventuality doesn't leave your family with more than sorrow or grief.

You want to do what you can to make sure that the financial stuff will be okay—or relatively okay. You'll do that by paying careful attention to three types of insurance:

- *Life Insurance*
- *Disability Insurance*
- *Health Insurance*

Life Insurance

Did you know that your chances of dying are 100 percent? Shocking! When you die, you want your family to continue living in the lifestyle they've been accustomed to. If you're a sole earner, or the primary breadwinner in the family, you have to take this responsibility incredibly seriously. If you haven't figured out your insurance needs, you need to do so immediately.

Before we get to the figuring of exactly how much life insurance you need, I should make clear that there are different types of insurance available. There are, essentially, two different types of life insurance policies: *term* and *cash value.* I'll explain these in some detail below, but as you read the following section, realize that cash-value polices suck. They're horrible for almost everyone. If you're not the sort who can afford some high-priced money manager for your vast holdings (and, really, would you be reading this book if you were) cash-value polices are not for you.

Term Life

The theory of term life is exceedingly simple. You, a person who's sure to die at some point, enters a contract with a company to pay a specific sum of money on a schedule—say monthly. In return for your payment, the company agrees to pay your beneficiaries a sum of money upon your death. The details of the policy will be guaranteed for a number of years, during which your premium (the amount you pay) and your benefit (the amount the insurance company pays out) are guaranteed. You stop making your payments, your beneficiaries get nothing. Payments in previous months or years mean nothing to the insurance company if you are not up to date.

Cash-Value Policy

A cash-value policy is a different animal altogether. It is really a savings and investment vehicle as well as a pure insurance policy. With cash-value policies, a portion of your money is put into an account where it gathers interest. Over time, that account grows, and if all goes stunningly well, that sum of money will be so large that you won't need to pay premiums anymore. So even if you stop paying into your policy, there will be money going to your beneficiaries. You, the policy holder, can even access the money in the account should you need it. There are some tax benefits to cash-value policies in that the money that you have in an investment account is tax-deferred as it grows.

But as I mentioned just a few paragraphs ago, cash-value policies are not so wonderful. With all of these features, why would that be? I'll give you the short answer—cost. Massive, absurd, blow-your-mind cost. Depending on the policies involved, you may pay between five to ten times as much to get the same benefit from a cash-value policy as you would from a term policy.

If some salesman tries to sell you on the cash-value policy, he's likely to tout the savings aspect associated with the policy. At this point, I want you to turn to the salesman, raising your arm over your head, and scream, "I do not need your lame savings plan. I invest myself. I Rule My Freakin' Retirement, dude (or dudess)!" Don't do this if you're embarrassed by drawing crowds, I'm not really the shy type—in case you haven't noticed by now—so it don't bother me. Either way, remember that your savings are yours and you're the best one to invest them wisely. You don't need or want an insurance company deciding where your money should be.

Salesmen involved in most insurance products—cash-value policies, annuities, and the like—are a pretty sleazy bunch, by and large. (Your cousin who sells insurance is the clear exception.) They push cash-value policies because they make the salesmen lots of dough. Lots of ka-chingos! The kind that ain't no good for you, my friend.

So just buy term life and be done with it. Okay?

How Much Life Insurance Do You Need?

If you go to insurance company Web sites, you'll often see very intricate tables and worksheets that help you determine how much term life you need. You can tackle a couple of these if you wish, but, in my opinion, they're not strictly necessary. A lot of financial planners recommend a really simple way to think about how much money you want in your benefit, and I agree with the approach.

You want your insurance, in the event of your death, to replace your income for the remainder of your working life. If you plan on working ten years till retirement and make $100,000, a $1 million policy is about right. Somewhat lower than this might be reasonable, you need to take a deep breath and think about what happens postmortem to your loved ones. If you have a spouse who's on an upward career path, or if you see some big reduction in spending on the horizon, then you can factor that in as well. You can also factor in Social Security's death benefit. If you've been paying into the Social Security system, your family will be entitled to benefits upon your demise. However, that sum will be very, very minimal if your spouse works.

My general feeling on this is that you don't want to screw with your family's comfort, so it's best to err on the side of a little too much coverage (or a lot). If you keep your policy to 80 to 100 percent of your future earnings, you should all be in good shape.

....
WAXIE'S TIP: Where to Buy

There are a bunch of online resources for finding a good price on term life insurance, such as selectquote.com. Comparison shopping has gotten very, very easy. But at the end of the day, you want to be buying insurance from one of the big reputable companies. Smaller companies have been known to go belly-up and leave people in horrible predicaments. Bigger, well-regarded companies are also less likely to have slimy practices. For example, you never want to enter into an insurance contract that allows the company to adjust the premium or cancel the policy should your health situation change. A policy should be *guaranteed renewable* and *noncancelable.*

Disability

Disability insurance replaces income that you lose in the event that, due to some serious health issue, you are unable to work. In the broadest view, there are two types of disability insurance: short- and long-term. Short-term will cover expenses for a few weeks, whereas long-term disability will cover a portion or all of your salary for a period of time.

Long-term policies range anywhere from five to ten years, and some will provide replacement income until you reach age 65. If you work for a large employer, it's likely that your benefits package includes some disability benefits. If you work for a small business or are self-employed, it's likely you've got nothing in the way of disability insurance.

WAXIE'S NOTE: Looking to Social Security

For those who have a significant (greater than ten-year) work history, Social Security does offer some disability benefits. This, however, is an option for the desperate. The benefits are meant to allow a subsistence living, and shouldn't even be considered as an option by anyone who had the money to buy a copy of this book.

The best option is to buy disability that replaces most (if not all) of your income until you're sixty-five. The logic is pretty simple—if you're unfortunate enough to be in such bad health that you can't work for five or ten years, the prospect of getting back to work at any point in your life are likely pretty small, at best. At worst, there's no chance you'll work again, at least not in a way that can provide any meaningful financial stability.

There are a few factors when considering what disability insurance you need.

■ *Elimination period.* This is the time from the onset of your injury till the start of your benefits payout. This could be anywhere between 30 and 90 days. The longer the elimination period, the less the insurance.

■ *Disability type.* This you need to look into carefully. Some policies will pay if you're not able to perform the tasks typical of your profession. Others take a narrower view. Make sure you understand how the policy you're considering defines disability.

■ *Permanence.* As I mentioned with health insurance, you want a policy that is noncancelable and guaranteed renewable.

Really, the best advice I can give in regard to disability insurance is to, first, check with your employer. Get into the details of what's offered. It may very well be enough to suit your needs. If you're self-employed, check with any professional organization that you belong to. Buying as part of a group is by far the best way to go.

Long-Term Care

Related to long-term disability policies are long-term care, which cover extended stays in nursing homes or home care. Policies vary widely here. Some cover periods of only a couple of years, while others are indefinite. The indefinite term ones aren't a whole lot more expensive, and so tend to be a better deal. When shopping for long-term care policies, it's extremely important to look at the definitions and see what makes one eligible for the policy.

And once again, you want to make sure the policy is guaranteed renewable.

Health Insurance

It's assumed in this chapter that you're covered by some good health insurance plan. At least, I very much hope that is the case. Most of you reading this book will be covered by your employer, and if you're not, you need to find another solution.

I just wanted to bring it up here briefly, because it's so important, but the specifics of health care—all the types of plans, what's available in given states, the role of Medicare and Medicaid—are so sprawling that it's beyond the scope of this book. Make sure, as with everything else (even when it comes to me) that you do your own due diligence so you are comfortable with whatever choice you make. It is, after all, *your* choice and your life (and death).

Quiz

1. **For most people, which form of life insurance is the better policy?**

   a. Term
   b. Cash-value
   Answer: a

2. **A policy that forbids the policy issuer from making changes to your insurance when your health situation changes is known by what term?**

   a. Noncancelable
   b. Guaranteed renewable
   c. Guaranteed rate
   d. Lifetime guaranteed
   Answer: a

3. **In disability insurance polices, what is the term used to describe the period of time that elapses between an injury and the start of the insurance payout?**

   a. Determination period
   b. Elimination period
   c. Interim period
   d. Vacant period
   Answer: b

4. **True or false: Social Security provides adequate replacement for income in the case of disability.**

   a. True
   b. False
   Answer: b

5. *When looking at life insurance, what should you examine to determine the payout of the policy?*

    a. Your annual salary

    b. The amount of debt you carry

    c. The amount you stand to earn for the rest of your working life

    d. The cost of your family's future obligations

    Answer: c

Chapter 8

Estate Planning

Okay, you just died. Sorry, it's ova, you sealed the deal, stick a fork in ya, dude or dudess! Sucks, but it's one of two things everyone on earth does, that we know of—birth and death. I guess there is the ole "eat, *&^%, and die" line, but you could make a case that the only thing we all really have in common is life and death. So, with that in mind, we all gotta do—estate planning!

Estate planning is a crucial part of your retirement plan—actually, it's a crucial part of your life plan—and part of estate planning is taking care of bizness while you are able to, so that you are prepared for the day when you're no longer able to make decisions for yourself—when you're completely incapacitated or dead. It's a lot of paperwork. You'll probably end up seeing a lawyer if you want to do it right—and that's even less fun than considering your own demise.

The key thing is that you want to make sure that your wishes are being carried out in an efficient and logical way. You don't want more than your share of money going to the tax man. I mean, I know we *all* love the tax man, but he has enough without getting money from you he shouldn't if you plan well—and you certainly don't want your loved ones spending time in court because you've failed to say exactly how your possessions should be divided.

In the area of estate planning there are a few general topics that you need to familiarize yourself with. But there's only so much I can cover here. Laws vary from state to state, and you need to be cognizant of what exactly is permitted in the state where you reside. Once you know the general terms and strategies, you need to see an estate planning lawyer to get yourself set up properly. The best I can do in this chapter is prep you for the meeting.

But before you even get to the paperwork, there are a couple of things that you can do that will ease the planning process. First off, you can take careful stock of your valuables—everything from IRAs to heirlooms. Just going through the jewelry drawer and deciding who would really appreciate that generations-old necklace will help you make decisions as you go along. The other thing that you should consider is talking to your heirs about your thoughts and decisions. One child may have a particular attachment to a possession that the other doesn't care so much about. You'll only know if you bring it up. If you opt not to enter in this conversation prior to finalizing your estate planning, you absolutely should do it once your will and trusts are in place. Explain your estate plans and the reasons for them to your heirs. It may save some hard feelings, and maybe even lawsuits down the road. You don't want your passing to be the genesis of hard feelings and legal action. Trust me on that one. I remember when my grandmother died as a kid, it was traumatic to begin with, but watching some of my adult relatives get a bit petty was not a pretty sight. Money and death of loved ones can make people do things they might normally not. Why stress an already stressful situation? You're being smart and considerate enough to plan your estate, you might as well finish the job the right way all around.

Taxes on Your Estate

If you want to save your heirs a bundle on estate taxes, you'll do them a favor by kicking the bucket in 2010. Why's that? Well, our funny government passed a law in 2004 that has been gradually increasing the amount that is exempt from estate taxes. In 2008, $2 million is exempt; in 2009, $3.5 million is exempt; in 2010, there's no estate tax at all. But here's the thing, this law is set to expire at that point, and in 2011, the exempt amount will revert to $1 million, unless Congress and the president extend the repeal.

WAXIE'S TIP

If ya gotta go, go in 2010!

Will

Everyone reading this page should have a will. A will describes in detail how your assets will be distributed upon your death. If you have dependent children, the will is where you decide who will become the children's guardian. You can find templates for wills online, but really you will be better off seeing a lawyer in your state and getting it done right.

Any assets that are not assigned within your will are considered to be in "probate"—a court will have to decide what happens to these assets. Avoiding probate is the key reason you want to make sure you set up your will carefully. It's also the reason you want to revisit your will on a semiregular basis.

If you have few assets, a will may be all you need, but those with significant amounts of money or property should consider setting up a trust.

Trusts

If you own property or have accounts worth more than $100,000, you should strongly consider setting up some type of trust. At its most basic, a trust is a legal entity that becomes the "owner" of property or money or other assets. A trustee (a person or financial institution) makes decisions for the trust. These decisions must be in the best interest of the *beneficiary* or *beneficiaries,* those who will benefit from the trust's assets. The trustee more or less has full control of the property in the trust, and is legally required to act in the beneficiary's interest. If the trustee acts irresponsibly, he is subject to lawsuits. Often a good friend or family member with financial savvy is set up as a trustee; other times a bank or financial institution is assigned the trustee's responsibility.

Trusts are very flexible and have some distinct advantages over a will in transferring your assets upon your death.

■ They often provide a way to avoid some estate taxes.

■ Trusts offer a more nuanced way of distributing your estate. For example, if you wanted to grant a sum of money to young grandchildren for their college education, you'd want to set up a trust that was very specific to that purpose. Or you could use a trust to set up specific use of a property among several people—a vacation house, for example.

■ Trusts are excellent vehicles for ensuring that specific assets go to different heirs over time. You may want your spouse to get a certain amount, while ensuring that your children get a percentage of your assets when appropriate.

■ A trust can be very useful in providing financial assistance for a relative who needs access to Medicare. Since the trust is the owner of the assets, the relative will not be disqualified from Medicare assistance.

■ Trusts are an excellent way to give large amounts of money or property to charity.

■ Trusts are useful in providing assistance to heirs who are either irresponsible or have limited ability to manage money. To offer a dramatic example, you probably wouldn't want to give a huge lump sum of money to an heir with a long-running drug dependency.

Each of the situations above requires a slightly different sort of trust. Though the basics of trusts are simple, there are many complex ways of setting them up, and the laws on what is permissible in trusts varies from state to state. If you think a trust is right for you, you should consult an attorney.

······················
WAXIE'S TIP

In trusts we trust! If you have substantial assets, setting one up is likely to be a good idea.

Choosing a Trustee

Being a trustee is a big responsibility. It's a burden that at first may seem like a logical job for a family member or friend. But before you ask someone to become a trustee, think about the impact the job might have on any relationship already existing between the beneficiary and trustee. Depending on how a trust is set up, the trustee may have broad latitude in how the money is invested and distributed. The beneficiary may strongly disagree with how the trustee is doing his job, and things can get ugly pretty quickly.

Banks can also be set up as trustees, but their services are usually expensive. A lot of trust experts are now recommending an arrangement in which a family member is the trustee but a bank is hired as an investment advisor to the trust.

······················
WAXIE'S TIP

Trust your trustee! They may have vast powers over your assets. Ya better make sure they got your back, baby!

The Living Will and Power of Attorney

A living will does not help distribute your assets, but rather sets forth your desires for your care should you be alive but unable to communicate them to those who are caring for you. A living will allows you to be very specific about the conditions you would want or would refuse. Perhaps the most common use of the living will is to specify a desire to refuse any heroic treatment while in a state of total mental incapacitation. You get to define the terms "heroic" and "total mental incapacitation" for yourself. At the very least, a living will lets your heirs know exactly how you'd proceed if you were aware of a grim condition. A living will also allows you to assign a health-care agent, someone who you've decided will make decisions when your living will is unclear.

The laws governing living wills vary from state to state, so consult an attorney when you want to draft one. While considering a living will, it's also important to consider creating a power of attorney for health care, which is another way of appointing an agent to look after your medical decisions. Note that a health-care power of attorney is distinct from a general power of attorney.

A general power of attorney assigns an agent to make decisions on your financial interest should you become incapacitated. This is an important step, because should you fail to appoint an agent power of attorney, a court would be assigned the role, which would come at significant cost.

When you go to an estate lawyer you should be aware that there are several types of powers of attorney that you will need to discuss.

- *Durable power of attorney.* A durable power of attorney allows the agent to make all decisions on all financial matters, and it goes into effect immediately upon signing the agreement. This gives the agent significant power. Theoretically, the agent could make decisions without your knowledge, even while you are competent enough to make your own decisions.

- *Limited power of attorney.* A limited power of attorney specifies a limited number of transactions the agent can make on your behalf. These arrangements are often made for business or real estate deals.

- *Springing power of attorney.* A springing power of attorney assigns the agent rights to make transactions when a level of incapacity is reached. This requires a medical determination of incapacity. Difficulty can arise in exercising the power of attorney if doctors feel differently than the beneficiaries or the agent. Even with all the paperwork in hand, a financial institution may deny the validity of a springing power of attorney. A good estate lawyer can discuss the limitations and dangers of this arrangement with you.

Potential Limits of Springing Power of Attorney

A close family friend was recently dealing with a completely incapacitated parent who had been fading for some time. The friend had a springing power of attorney, and should have been able to make all decisions regarding the disposition of funds in the parent's accounts. But things didn't go well. One of the banks that she had to deal with steadfastly refused to let my friend make any decisions about one of the accounts, despite the medical certification. It was a difficult and extremely stressful encounter. With the parent unable to get to the bank, and not competent to make a decision, it seemed as though the bank was putting itself in a position to just hold the money, without anyone ever having access to it. It was a total mess that required a lot of screaming and letters from lawyers threatening legal action. And even a threat from a lawyer comes at a substantial cost. The situation could very well have ended up in court. My friend wished that she had simply had her name put on all the accounts. That way the money was as much hers as it was the parent's. This sort of an arrangement won't be one that everyone wants to enter, but if you have someone you really trust to look after your financial decisions, it may be a better idea to put that person as a co-owner of major accounts when you're getting to the point where you can predict that your capacity will decline.

WAXIE'S TIP

Dying ain't fun for you or your loved ones. Make the transition as easy as possible for them. They don't need the hassles of dealing with your demise and the financial mess you'll leave behind if you don't plan your estate!

Quiz

1. *Which of the following are advantages of trusts?*

   a. They provide a way to give large sums to charities

   b. They allow for nuanced distribution of funds to family members

   c. They allow for distribution over time

   d. They allow for avoidance of some estate taxes

   Answer: a, b, c, d

2. *Which of the following describes a power of attorney that starts at the moment the papers are signed?*

   a. Durable power of attorney

   b. Limited power of attorney

   c. Springing power of attorney

   Answer: a

3. *Which of the following describes a power of attorney that starts when a level of incapacity is reached?*

   a. Durable power of attorney

   b. Limited power of attorney

   c. Springing power of attorney

   Answer: a

4. *In a living will, the person who will oversee your care if you should become incapacitated is known as:*

    a. The decider

    b. The medical determination arbiter

    c. The health-care custodian

    d. Health-care agent

    Answer: d

5. *True or false: Banks and other institutions will readily accept a power of attorney document.*

    a. True

    b. False

    Answer: b

Part II

Mastering the Tools

Chapter 9

Stocking Away Your Cash

Okay, here's a true shocker for ya.

The U.S. government wants you to be ready for retirement! It's not an altruistic desire, believe me. The fact is that it's better for the country as a whole if you and your peers can take care of yourselves in your golden years. It would be expensive for taxpayers if many elderly people became destitute and required a variety of forms of government assistance beyond Social Security. It would also be pretty depressing for us as a society. We all know what a hot topic the potential lack of Social Security money for baby boomers and beyond has become. No one wants a bunch of us old people picketing the White House anytime soon, it's not good public relations!

So, to encourage people to prepare for retirement, the government has created all sorts of regulations and incentives that steer people toward saving. The government uses one basic tool to move you toward fiscal responsibility: They'll save you some tax burden if you do save, and whack you in the kneecaps with a big-ass baseball bat if you don't. *Bam!*

Learning about this stuff can be annoying. You have to familiarize yourself with a bunch of acronyms and shorthand form sections of federal tax law. Plus, you'll have to consult some charts and maybe do a little math. It's a drag, I know. But it's worth it. You might save thousands per year by taking full advantage of retirement accounts. So take the time; you'll be glad you did. And that's part of the message of this book overall: *You* need to take the time, take the initiative, and take *responsibility* for your retirement! I read somewhere that the average male over the age of twenty-one spends roughly five to seven hours a week either thinking about or actually viewing pornography. Women do their own "thing"; some view porno the same or more than men do. *Everyone* needs to take a couple of those wasted hours a week and do some leg work so that you can live the life of Riley in the so-called latter part of your life!

The Alphanumeric Soup

Federal tax law provides several methods for saving for retirement while avoiding taxes. Each of these accounts comes with a particular set of tax advantages and limitations.

Plans From the Workplace

401(k)

The most common vehicle for savings for many workers is the 401(k). This is a tax-deferred account that you'll get through your job. The essentials of the 401(k) work like this: Your employer will ask you if you want to contribute to the company retirement plan—a 401(k). When you say that you would (which you *better!*), the employer withholds some of your earnings and puts it directly into your account. The monies that are placed in your account are taken from your pretax earnings so you pay no federal, state, or local taxes on that money. That's a good thing—a very good thing. But, of course, the government will want its piece of the action eventually. When you withdraw money from your 401(k) (known as a disbursement), you'll pay taxes on the money you take: The IRS will treat that money as if it's normal income. (See the sidebar on penalties to see the limitations you'll have on withdrawing your money from your 401(k).)

Some large investment institutions, like T. Rowe Price, Fidelity, and Vanguard, will usually maintain the account. Most of the time the account will offer a limited number of mutual funds from which you'll be required to choose.

WAXIE'S NOTE

Your employer's 401(k) may not offer the best set of funds in the world, but you'll have to make do. It's sad, but you got no choice, baby, so make the best of it. We'll talk about picking the best mutual funds in chapter 10.

There are limits to the amount you can deposit in your 401(k). Federal law limited your contributions to $15,500 in 2007 and 2008. Be aware that most employers put their own limits on the amounts that can be contributed to a 401(k). Often, a company will limit employees to 10 percent of their salary. Within the limits allowed by law, you can decide to put away as much as you want.

WAXIE'S TIP

Talk to your employer's benefits administrator to learn about the specifics of your retirement plan. Some companies offer to match the amount you contribute to a 401(k) fund. Or they'll throw in some percentage of that amount. That is free money, and you want to make sure you get every dime of it. You wouldn't believe how many people don't take advantage of this, preferring instead to spend the money they could be saving (and forfeiting the *free* money) on "stuff" they really don't need.

WAXIE'S SIDEBAR: Penalties

Nearly every retirement plan, from 401(k)s to IRAs, has associated penalties for withdrawing money before the age of 59.5—and that's in addition to the normal taxes you'd pay on the disbursement. This is the government's way of keeping you from treating these funds like another vacation account. They want you to deposit and hold the money, which, as I've stated, is a very good idea. However, there are some circumstances where you can withdraw money penalty-free, but you will have to pay tax on the withdrawal. The government has defined some hardships for which there are no penalties. These include medical expenses, funeral expenses, back-tax payments, and foreclosure. Basically, if your life is falling apart, the government will give a "sucka" a break. About the only *happy* circumstance that will allow penalty-free withdrawal is the first-time purchase of a house. A first-time home buyer can take $10,000 penalty-free. Check with your benefits administrator at work or the institution that holds your IRA for details on the paperwork of an early withdrawal.

The Bottom Line

What's the bottom line on 401(k)s? You should put as much money in your company's 401(k) as you can. The tax advantages alone make it an incredible bargain. Think of it this way: If you make $65,000 per year and make your employer's maximum contribution of 10 percent to your 401(k), you'll be shielding $6,500 from taxes. Assuming you pay 30 percent in taxes, you'll keep the tax man from $1,900 of your money. Should there be a matching contribution, you'd make even more. Some employers match as much as fifty cents on every dollar of contribution, which would give you another $3,700 to invest. That's a very nice free ka-chingo! We like that, so should you.

Note that when you leave the employer who has administered your 401(k), you'll want to take the money with you. Set up a rollover IRA at any investment house, and then transfer the money into that.

You'll also need to do some paperwork from your benefits administrator. Generally, the paperwork for rolling over a 401(k) into an IRA takes about twenty minutes to complete, even for people like myself who are horrendous at paperwork.

Roth 401(k)

In a traditional 401(k), an employer withholds pretax dollars, placing them in an account. The money grows in the investment account and is only taxed as income when the saver removes funds from the account after age 59.5 without penalty. A Roth 401(k) is slightly different in that the money that is put in the account comes from post-tax dollars.

Why would you even consider contributing post-tax dollars when you can use pretax income? The Roth version of the 401(k) comes with its own tax benefits that are probably greater than those of the normal 401(k). There are no taxes required upon disbursement of the money, provided that the money has been in the account for five years and that the holder of the account is at least 59.5 years old. (See the section on Traditional Accounts Versus Roth Accounts to hear more about the advantages of Roth accounts.)

The total contribution to your Roth 401(k) and traditional 401(k) cannot be greater than $15,500 in 2007 and $16,000 in 2008, though those over 50 can add an additional $5,000 each year.

403(b)

You don't need to read about 403(b)s unless you work for a nonprofit or educational organization—or you're a minister. Nonprofits are generally smaller and have less money to put into the maintenance of retirement plans. To help these organizations offer their employees some way of preparing for retirement the tax code writers came up with the 403(b). In practice, a 403(b) will be nearly identical to a 401(k). The major difference is that the 403(b) requires less paperwork (almost none) from the organization involved.

The same limits of the 401(k) apply to the 403(b), and there is a

Roth version of the 403(b), if the organization opts to offer it. Again, this isn't something most of us will need to learn about, but for those that do, there ya go!

Small-Business Plans

Those running small businesses and sole proprietorships have a variety of tax-friendly plans to choose from. If you work for a small business, you may have the opportunity to join one of these plans. If you own a small business, you can start one of the following plans for you and your employees. You should. Trust me when I tell you that your employees will appreciate it, and that'll show in their work ethic more than likely. In life, truly, one hand does wash the other, and my experience is that the more generous you are in your life, the more you'll make. It's said that for every dollar of charity you do, you'll get it back times twelve over the long haul. I've experienced that in my life so I speak from experience. Try it, you may find ya like giving back a little of what you got. I think many of us spend far too much time *not* thinking about others who have less than we do. We're discussing retirement here when much of the world worries about what they are going to be able to eat tomorrow. We're very lucky, we should be grateful, and we should be charitable. I try to be, and I try to teach my two beautiful little girls that as well. Yes, they have done charity work, starting at age 4! And ya know what? They enjoyed it. So will you!

....
WAXIE'S TIP

Have a lucrative small business? Good for you. You have some options for your retirement plans. In addition to the plans listed in this book (SIMPLE-IRA, SEP-IRA, individual 401(k)), you may have the option of starting an individual pension plan. This sort of plan allows you to put a lot money out of reach of the IRS—as much as $100,000 per year. Have a talk with your accountant to see if an individual defined-benefits plan is right for you.

SIMPLE-IRA

Small businesses, those with one hundred or fewer employees, can offer a SIMPLE-IRA (Savings Incentive Match Plan). A SIMPLE-IRA has smaller contribution limits than a 401(k); employees can contribute no more than $10,500 per year, with an added $2,500 in catch-up contributions available to those over 50. An employer is required to match a small amount of the contributions employees make to a SIMPLE plan.

Contributions to SIMPLE-IRAs are tax-deductible, and any gains in your account are tax-deferred; you're taxed on the money as you withdraw it from the account. As with a 401(k), there's a 10 percent penalty if the money is removed from the account before age 59.5.

SEP

SEP stands for Simplified Employee Pension and is the retirement savings vehicle of choice for independent contractors, sole proprietorships, and very small businesses. SEP plan holders can usually contribute 20 percent of their income up to $44,000 per year in 2009. The exact amount you can contribute depends on your income. To come up with the exact number you'll be able to contribute, you'll need to get IRS Publication 560, *Retirement Plans for Small Business* (http://www.irs.gov/pub/irs-pdf/p560.pdf), which covers SEPs, SIMPLEs, and some other plans. The tables will help you determine what you can contribute.

The money you put in your SEP is tax-deductible. Money in your SEP receives the same treatment as a 401(k): Taxes are deferred until you start withdrawing the money at age 59.5, at which time disbursements are treated as income.

As I'm writing this chapter in 2008, there is no Roth SEP option, and there's no talk of one becoming available any time in the near future.

Individual 401(k)

The individual 401(k) is for self-employed persons with no employees other than a spouse. The major benefit of the individual 401(k) over a SEP is that it allows some people to deposit more money at a lower income level. For example, a person operating as a sole-proprietorship and making $150,000 per year, could put $30,000 into a SEP in 2008. But using a combination of salary deferral and profit-sharing, the same $150,000 income could be used to put $44,000 into an individual 401(k) and SEP.

Maintaining an individual 401(k) requires more administration and paperwork than a SEP—a lot more. You'll need to structure your salary so that you can take appropriate amounts as an "employee" of your company and then another amount as a matching contribution. Talking with an accountant before going down the 401(k) road is probably the way to go. Again, you need to stay on top of your future, and part of that is having a good team to help you. A good accountant is a good start. I rely heavily on my accountant to help me manage my financial future (and my present as well). Make sure you have a good one. How do you find a good accountant? Ask for references and check them. And then interview them and see if the two of you see eye to eye before settling on someone just because you are lazy.

....

WAXIE'S TIP

An individual 401(k) can be configured as a Roth plan, which should be an exciting opportunity for the self-employed who are doing pretty well. Up to $20,000 per year can get the Roth treatment in an individual IRA.

Keogh Plan

If you're fortunate enough to own a business that's doing very, very well—say you have at least a few employees and you're pulling in over $200,000 a year—you might want to consider a Keogh plan. A Keogh is what's known as a qualified plan, meaning that it's subject to some specific regulations of federal law, namely ERISA, the Employee Retirement Income Security Act. ERISA covers 401(k)s and pensions for larger companies by defining a set of rules that ensure that money stocked away for retirement isn't pilfered or exploited by the companies keeping the plan. Plans governed by ERISA, such as Keoghs, take time and money to administer.

Keoghs allow small business owners to put a big percentage of their income in tax-deferred accounts while offering a smaller percentage to employees. Keoghs come in many varieties.

If you're in the fortunate position where you could even consider a Keogh, you should spend a good long time running numbers with your accountant.

················

WAXIE'S TIP

When looking at the income restrictions for contributions to IRAs, the IRS is interested in what it calls the modified adjusted gross income, or MAGI. The MAGI is essentially your income from a variety of sources minus some deductions.

Individual (Non-Workplace) Plans

Outside of the workplace, there are some options for shielding money from the feds. Most have heard of these vehicles, called IRAs, or individual retirement accounts. You can setup an IRA at any investment house or even many banks. Unlike the workplace plans discussed in the previous section, you set up and maintain an IRA by yourself.

There are two basic flavors of IRAs, the traditional IRA and the Roth IRA. Contributions to a traditional IRA may be tax-deductible, given certain income restrictions. Money within the IRA is taxed as income when withdrawn from the account after age 59.5. Prior to age 59.5, there is a 10 percent penalty, if an exception does not apply.

Most of the readers of this book will be able to deposit, currently, at least $5,000 in an IRA. Add another thousand to the contribution limits if you're 50 or older. However, if you had a really bad year, and you made less than $4,000, your maximum contribution will be 100 percent of your salary. For married couples, an additional $4,000 can be put into a spouse's account if the total income for the couple is at least $8,000.

There are two factors that will determine whether your IRA contribution is partially or wholly tax-deductible: your involvement in an employer-sponsored retirement plan and your income.

Employer-sponsored plans include pensions and profit-sharing plans. The easiest way to determine whether or not you're contributing to such a plan is to look at your most recent W-2. Look for the box that says Retirement Plan. If there's an X in the box, you're contributing.

Generally, the limits on tax deductions are shown on the next page.

If you're entitled to a partial deduction, you need to read chapter 5 of IRS Publication 590, *Individual Retirement Accounts (IRAs)*, to see the exact deduction you're entitled to.

Roth IRA

A Roth IRA, like its cousin, the Roth 401(k), has the same contribution limits as a traditional IRA—$4,000 per year in 2007 and $5,000 in 2008, with an additional $1,000 available to those 50 or older. The difference between a Roth IRA and a traditional IRA is the tax treatment. Contributions to a Roth are never tax-deductible. However, when funds are disbursed after age 59.5, there is no taxation at all.

Generally, single persons making less than $95,000 and married people making less than $150,000 can contribute the full amount to a Roth IRA. Individuals making more than $110,000 and couples making more than $160,000 cannot fund a Roth. If you don't fall

TABLE 9-1.   Allowable deductions for IRA contributions

MARITAL STATUS	CONTRIBUTING TO A BENEFIT PLAN	SPOUSE CONTRIBUTING TO BENEFIT PLAN	INCOME	DEDUCTION
Married (filing jointly)	No	Yes	Less than $150,000	Full deduction
Married (filing jointly)	No	Yes	Between $150,000 and $160,000	Partial deduction
Married (filing jointly)	No	Yes	More than $160,000	No deduction
Married (filing jointly)	No	No	Any amount	Full deduction
Married (filing jointly)	Yes	N/A	$70,000 or less	Full deduction
Married (filing jointly)	Yes	N/A	Between $70,000 and $80,000	Partial deduction
Married (filing jointly)	Yes	N/A	More than $80,000	No deduction
Single	No		Any amount	Full deduction
Single	Yes		$50,000 or less	Full deduction
Single	Yes		More than $60,000	No deduction
Single	Yes		Between $50,000 and $60,000	Partial deduction

into either of these categories (you individually make between $95,000 and $110,000 or as a couple you make between $150,000 and $160,000), you can make a partial contribution. See IRS Publication 590, chapter 2, to figure out the exact contribution you can make.

WAXIE'S NOTE

The funding limits given for traditional and Roth IRAs ($4,000 for 2007, $5,000 for 2008) reflect the total amount you can contribute to these plans. You can't put $4,000 in a traditional IRA, and then throw another $4,000 in a Roth.

Traditional Accounts Versus Roth Accounts

Now that you can give your 401(k)s and IRAs the Roth treatment, the obvious questions arise as to which is better: the immediate tax advantage of a traditional 401(k) and IRA where you save money up front, or the Roth, where you pay more to start but have a tax advantage in retirement?

There are a lot of factors to consider: the time the money will be in an account, the expected return on the account, your current tax bracket, and your likely tax bracket in retirement, to name just a few. It's tough to define every element that goes into the equation, but I'll give you this general rule: You should probably be looking to put what you can in a Roth unless you have a specific reason not to. If you can only max out your 401(k) or IRA contributions by saving with pretax dollars, then do that. You're much better off finding some tax advantage rather than none. The other major case where traditional accounts are preferable to Roths is if you think your tax rate will be much lower in retirement than at the time you're making contributions.

But most of the readers of this book, I think, are looking for a comfortable retirement with an income that is pretty similar (or better) to what they've enjoyed in their work lives. For these folks, the Roth is the way to go.

There is a further question of whether it's worth converting an existing IRA to a Roth, which is doable if you meet the income restrictions. As of the writing of this book, you needed to have income under $100,000 for a single person or $150,000 for a couple to be eligible for the conversion. However, there may be some workarounds for those with higher incomes. The income restriction for conversions is set to expire in 2010, so you might be able to make the conversion then.

In doing research for this book, I found the blogger "fivecentnickle," (http://www.fivecentnickel.com) who pointed out that this opens up an opportunity for wealthy investors to make use of the Roth IRA (which was really a vehicle to assist people of more moderate means). A person making a high income could make non-tax-deductible contributions to a standard IRA, then convert it to a Roth in 2010. If the law doesn't change, people could do this year after year, taking full advantage of all the Roth has to offer.

To convert a traditional IRA to a Roth IRA, you must pay the taxes you avoided initially, and when you do this on an IRA or a SEP-IRA that you've been funding for years, it can seem like a pretty healthy chunk of change. Still, it's probably worth it, though you really want to be paying your taxes with money that is outside the IRAs. That is, you don't want your retirement account to take a 30 percent hit at the moment you convert. You want to pay that 30 percent out of a brokerage or bank account so that the full sum that was in your traditional IRA makes its way into your Roth. Check out the Roth Conversion Calculator at InvestSafe to get a better idea if a Roth conversion is for you: http://www.investsafe.com/development/calculators/Roth Transfer.html.

The Annuity Mess

Perhaps the single most confusing area of retirement planning concerns investments known as annuities. There are several types of annuities, and it's vital to know the differences between them if you're considering purchasing this sort of investment. The overarching rule when it comes to annuities is this: Assume you want nothing to do with them unless and until you're absolutely convinced that a certain annuity fits a specific financial goal. As I mentioned in chapter 1, there are hucksters in the annuity world. Seniors are often sold annuities that are totally inappropriate for them. Even administrators of retirement funds are tricked into buying bad annuity plans. The commissions on annuity sales are so high that salesmen will cram them down your throat. Consider yourself warned. Be careful.

Insurance and mutual fund companies sell a few types of annuities. Actually, this is a vast understatement. There seem to be dozens of types of annuities, each with a set of mind-boggling options. But in general annuities are classified as being either *variable* or *fixed*.

Variable (Tax-Deferred) Annuities

A few fortunate readers of this book will encounter a problem of excess; they'll make so much that they'll max out all the tax advantages we've talked about so far in this account. They'll have made the legal maximum $15,500 contribution to their 401(k), and they probably won't be eligible for IRA contributions—their income is too high. Those lucky few may find an investment counselor trying to talk them into a variable, tax-deferred annuity.

What is a variable, tax-deferred annuity? It's a grouping of mutual funds wrapped within an insurance policy. The return on this annuity will depend on the underlying funds; that's why it's called "variable." Depending on the variable annuity you buy, when you're ready to get the benefit of your investment, you can choose monthly payments for a specific period of time (maybe twenty years), or a lump sum, or payments for life.

The insurance wrapper usually guarantees a death benefit. If you die before you receive any money, your beneficiary will receive a specified sum, usually the amount of your original purchase. Make sure to look at the fine print of the benefit so you know exactly how any death benefit works once you've started taking payments from the annuity.

The first thing to understand is that the tax treatment of variable annuities isn't all that great: It doesn't approach what you can get out of a 401(k) or an IRA (either traditional or Roth). Your contributions aren't tax-deductible, and your payments are taxable as income. The only real advantage is that any gains in your account are tax-deferred until the time of payment. That is, your investment is not taxed while it compounds over time. That's usually a pretty meager advantage over a regular broker's account, where you're subject to taxes from capital gains and disbursements. You'll have to hold a variable annuity for a good long time—as long as fifteen or twenty years—to see any real advantage from it.

During that period your money is locked up. There are often early withdrawal fees of up to 6 or 7 percent (in addition to the 10 percent penalty you'd pay for disbursing money prior to age 59.5). Those withdrawal fees decrease over time, but, still, they're egregious. This is where seniors are often tripped up. They buy an annuity with dreadful early withdrawal penalties at a time when they really need access to their cash. Then, when they desperately need to get some money out, they get absolutely hammered.

If all this weren't enough, you need to consider the other fees that come with the annuities. Remember, mutual funds are at the center of these investments, so you're going to pay all the management fees of the underlying funds. In addition, there's a separate fee for the insurance wrapper part of the annuity, usually around 1 percent.

So in essence, if you opt for a variable annuity, you'll usually be sacrificing a full percentage point of interest in return for a minimal tax advantage. During the time you hold the annuity, your money's inaccessible and subject to big fees should you wish to get at it. Sounds awesome!

I'm a trader; I've made my money by moving investments to where they can make me money. In the rest of this book, I'm going to give you some tools you need to do the same. Tying up money for the sake of guaranteeing a minimal return is not what *Rule Your Freakin' Retirement* is about. It's about taking charge and *truly* being the king of your destiny, the *ruler* of your retirement!

Fixed and Life Annuities

With a fixed annuity, a purchaser plunks down a sum of money with an insurance company for the guarantee of getting monthly payments for either a specified period (fixed-term annuity) or the rest of the person's life (life annuity). The money invested in the annuity grows at a fixed rate. If the purchaser of a fixed-term annuity dies while time remains on the policy, the remaining monies go the heir in a single payment. (This could cause tax issues for the heir.)

When the money in a fixed annuity is paid out, the tax treatment is a little odd. Some portion of your payment will be treated as your principal, the amount you paid initially. That quantity won't be taxed. The remainder will be taxed as ordinary income. At a certain time, the annuity will have paid out the entirety of your original investment, and from that time on, everything you get from the annuity will be taxable.

Whereas the variable tax-deferred annuities are generally pretty poor investments except under very specific circumstances, fixed annuities do serve a legitimate purpose. A fixed term annuity can guarantee a senior a certain level of income for the remainder of his or her life, which could relieve a great mental burden for those who are worried about running out of money. Furthermore, a good fixed term annuity can be a pretty decent investment as far as return rates go.

A Final Warning

Given the breadth of annuity offerings out there, they can be immensely confusing. Different companies use different terms to describe similar things, so comparing annuities accurately can be really hard.

I've done a fair amount of research into the current annuity offerings, and it seems that Vanguard is a really good place to start looking for one. Their fees are low and their offerings are more straightforward than many. So if you think an annuity is right for you, start at vanguard.com and move on from there. *Never* buy an annuity from a company that seems the slightest bit shady.

WAXIE'S FINAL BARB

Confused? Overwhelmed? Take it a day (and a chapter) at a time! You own this book, you Rule Your Freakin' Retirement! Own it.

Quiz

1. *In 2008, what is the maximum that can be contributed to a 401(k)?*

   a. $12,000
   b. $14,200
   c. $15,500
   d. $18,400
   Answer: c

2. *Which of the following is a "qualified" small business play?*

   a. SEP
   b. SIMPLE-IRA
   c. Keogh
   d. Roth IRA
   Answer: c

3. *True or false: Roth IRA contributions are tax exempt.*

   a. True

   b. False

   Answer: b

4. *True or false: For those who qualify, a Roth is a better instrument than a traditional IRA.*

   a. True

   b. False

   Answer: a

5. *Put the following account types in order, from those you should fund first, to those you should fund last:*

   a. 401(k)

   b. Variable annuity

   c. IRA

   Answer: a, c, b

Chapter 10

Mutual Funds—The Good, the Mediocre, and the Downright Horrible

There are three things that are a given in life: death, taxes, and people who tell me they are not in the stock market, yet have, either by choice or because it's somehow forced on them through a union or job, a mutual fund or two in their 401(k). Truth is, you'd be hard-pressed to find a single person who has saved for retirement who does not have some money in mutual funds. Most 401(k)s are built on mutual funds, and they are far and away the most common investment choice for holders of IRAs. Mutual funds may be a good or bad thing for you, depending largely on the funds you've selected. But before I teach you how to look critically at mutual funds, it's worth taking a step back and looking at the basics: what mutual funds are and their purported advantages.

Mutual Fund Basics

So what exactly is a mutual fund? In the simplest terms a mutual fund is a grouping of similar investments. A stock mutual fund, for example, is a collection of a number of stocks. A bond mutual fund is a collection of bonds. Usually, mutual funds are designed so that investors have exposure to a particular sector of the market. A large-cap fund, for example, holds stock in many of the largest publicly traded companies in the country. A foreign-markets fund will look beyond the United States to different areas of the world for investments. We'll look at the most important sectors of the mutual fund marketplace later in this chapter. Investment companies have created thousands of funds covering every conceivable portion of the market. Funny as it may seem, there are now far more mutual funds than there are publicly traded stocks.

You can buy mutual funds just about anywhere these days. Your 401(k), if you have one, will likely give you a few funds to choose from. If you have an IRA or a brokerage account outside of your work-sponsored accounts, at a place like Schwab or Merrill Lynch, it may offer hundreds of funds from a variety of sources. All you have to do is tell your broker, through a phone call or a Web site, which fund you want to buy in what quantity. The fund will have a given price per share, like a stock, and your order will be filled at the close of the trading day. (Unlike stocks, all mutual fund transactions are executed at the close of a trading day. More on this later.) Then you hope that your shares gain value over time, and you can sell the fund for a profit. You may also make money through dividends and capital gains distributions.

For investors, the greatest advantage of mutual funds is that they offer an easy way to diversify. Buy into a mutual fund and you will have exposure to dozens of different stocks. If one or two of them have a bad week or quarter or year, it won't be a disaster for you, because many of the other stocks in the fund will (hopefully) do better. Creating a similarly diverse portfolio on your own would require researching and buying dozens of individual stocks. Most ordinary investors don't have the energy or expertise to keep up with the ups and downs of various companies. So a mutual fund is a relatively quick and easy way to get broad exposure.

Best Thing Ever?

Talk to most financial planners, and they'll nearly swoon when they talk about mutual funds, telling you that they are, without question, the best possible investments for nearly everyone. I'm not as sanguine. Mutual funds have their problems. I think you should understand my concerns with mutual funds before we go on with the rest of this chapter.

Investor Ennui

Mutual funds tend to make investors lazy. You buy a fund through your 401(k) or IRA and then you just hold it. That's what most investment advisors tell you to do: Just wait and make money as the market inevitably rises over the years and decades. But what if the market doesn't rise indefinitely? There's no guarantee that the market will go up forever at historic rates. If you were to manage your accounts more actively, you'd be better able to react to downswings in the market.

Even if you happen to believe in the broad market's steady and inevitable climb (I don't) and think that mutual funds are the best possible way ever to take advantage of it, you can still be lazy with mutual funds. Some people think that by simply investing in a few funds, they're as diversified as they need to be. That's not necessarily the case. If you're not really examining the funds in which you're invested, you might be invested in two or three funds that hold nearly identical stocks. You might feel that you're well protected from a downturn in one sector of the market, but then find that your portfolio takes a serious dive when the energy or technology sector takes a beating.

Somewhat Inflexible Investment

When you want to buy a mutual fund, you put in an order with your broker, either over the phone or online. That order won't be filled until the close of the trading day. That is, by law, how mutual funds work. All the trading, in or out, is done at the close of business. The exact price of the fund isn't determined until the end of the day, when the funds can see how their holdings have done that day and price their shares appropriately (more on the pricing of funds later).

I come from the world of trading—I've made my money by getting in and out of investments with some pretty precise timing. This isn't an option for mutual funds. But the truth is that in your retirement accounts there's a limited amount of trading you can do anyway. You can't trade in or out of a single stock more than once a day in an IRA, and you can only make one dollar in trades per day for every dollar in your account. For example, if you have $100,000 in your IRA, you can only make $100,000 worth of trades. In a regular trading account you can usually get 4 to 1 margin, thus enabling you to trade $400,000 with your $100,000.

Potential Tax Liabilities

You don't need to read this section if you're investing your funds in an IRA, 401(k), or other tax-deferred account. But if you're putting money into mutual funds in a normal brokerage account, you should be aware that many mutual funds aren't as tax friendly as others. You need to read the prospectus. Some mutual fund managers turn over their portfolio of funds frequently, creating taxable capital gains when a stock is sold at a profit. That said, there are some tax-friendly funds, which I'll talk more about later.

A 1 Percent Fleecing

The single greatest problem with mutual funds is that they take money from you and put money in the hands of stupidly wealthy investment bankers and fund managers. It costs money to create and manage mutual funds—and that's money that you're going to pay.

We'll talk more about the pricing of the funds and fund management fees as we move on with the chapter. Right now, I want you to think about what you could potentially save if you were to avoid mutual funds and their fees altogether. For the sake of this example, assume that you have $25,000 in an IRA and that you're investing in stocks that collectively have returned 9 percent annually over a thirty-year period. How much would you be giving up if you were to pay a 1 percent fund management fee? The numbers are pretty astonishing. Take a look at Figure 10.1 to see what happens to your money.

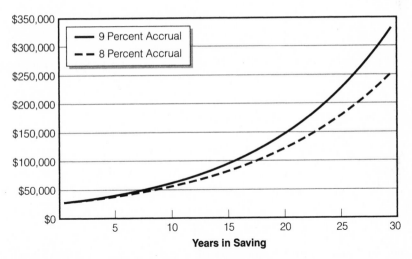

Figure 10.1   Small fees make a big difference

After thirty years, $25,000 would get you $331,691 at 9 percent; at 8 percent, your total would be $251,566. So over thirty years, you'd be giving up an astonishing $80,000. That's a *lot* of money. And this is a fraction of what you'll be paying over the course of your retirement planning because, if you're doing things right, you'll have a whole lot more money saved up.

....
WAXIE'S TIP

Please, don't give up money where you don't need to. You work way too hard for it, and the fund managers don't work nearly hard enough. 'Nuff said!

Did Someone Say, "Fees"?

In the section above, I showed the effect that management fees could have on your return. Depending on the fund, the management fee may be only the beginning of the expenses you encounter. As you research available funds, you'll run into the following types of fees:

- *Loads.* A load is an expense you incur either when you buy a fund (a front-end load) or sell a fund (back-end load). Most of the time, the load is given as a commission to the sales agent. Some funds charge as much as 5 percent up front as a broker's commission. If you have a financial advisor who pushes you toward a load fund, you need to start asking some tough questions about that person's objectives.

- *Redemption.* A fee charged to investors who sell their fund shares within a certain period of time after the original purchase date (often 30 or 60 or 90 days).

- *12b-1.* These fees are for marketing and disbursement. The catchy name comes from a section of the Securities and Exchange Commission code, which mandates that funds spell out these expenses clearly.

Trust *That* Guy?

Remember a couple of pages back when I talked about the hundreds of thousands you can end up paying in fund administration fees? I thought so. It sounds totally ridiculous, but I have to acknowledge that a fund manager could actually make a pretty good argument for charging these fees. Mr. Fund Manager, fresh from lunch at Le Cirque, might say that, yes, his services aren't cheap, but he's performing a highly valuable service. His knowledge of the markets allows him to invest for you in ways you couldn't possibly duplicate. And, in fact, his fees will more than pay for themselves, as his deft trading will keep you earning great returns— much higher than you could have ever possibly achieved yourself. He's a market professional, after all, and you—well, you do that thing you do, and you don't know much about the markets at all.

Okay, fine. It's sound reasoning. We pay too much for all kinds of competent professionals—from barbers to electricians—so why not for something as vital as investment management? In fact, there is a really good reason: Most fund managers just plain suck, or worse!

By saying this I'm not expressing some crazy anti-fund-manager bias. I'm sure many of these guys are nice people who have done decent things with their gobs of cash. Their pony farms and Hampton homes are gorgeous. I really have nothing against them. But, as a group, they're not very good at what they do. This isn't bigotry. This is an objective, measurable fact.

As I mentioned earlier, most funds stick to one market segment. A fund may be linked to foreign stocks or it may be linked to an industry sector. Study after study has found that the vast majority of funds— as much as 80 percent—underperform the sectors to which they're linked. Often they do just slightly better than the industry as a whole, or maybe slightly worse. But when you factor in management fees, they do not do well at all.

A Bad Fund in All Its Glory

Want to make 14 percent on your retirement investments? Of course you do. I mean, who wouldn't? And that's exactly what Dominant Global Financial's World Beater Fund delivers, according to its Web site and marketing literature. (Note: Dominant Global Financial doesn't exist; but I did base the World Beater Fund on an existing fund. I changed the name to avoid getting sued by some nasty and litigious people.)

The World Beater Fund prominently advertises its return rate over the past two years: 14.25 percent in the last year, and 11.5 percent in the year preceding. Its portfolio includes a bunch of truly esoteric, nearly unheard-of stocks, like Microsoft, General Electric, and Wells Fargo. Okay, I could probably think of those stocks myself, but these guys must be doing something right. After all, 14 percent!

But look a little deeper and you'll see that the World Beater Fund is part of the large growth sector—a major fund category that includes many funds that invest in large companies that have larger than average investment return potential. Information from my broker shows that the sector did pretty well over that period of time. In fact, the average fund in the sector made 16 percent in the previous year and about 10 percent the year before that.

Things start to get kind of fishy when I look at the fees charged by the fund. The management fees: 2.6 percent. Just in case you missed it, I'll give that number again: *2.6 percent.* So all those great numbers they gave about their return look a lot less wonderful now: 11.5, instead of 14 percent. Oh, and there's also a 0.25 percent 12b-1 fee.

All this—nearly 3 percent in fees—for the sake of owning GE and Microsoft! You've gotta be kidding me! But wait, there's more. The fund's manager is very active, so having this fund in a brokerage account would lose you another percentage point in taxes.

By investing in this fund, with its superamazing returns, you'd underperform the market by *5 percent!* This fund, by any measure, sucks.

Are Mutual Funds Useful?

Given all this mutual fund bashing that started this chapter, you might be thinking that I'm going to steer you away from funds. But that's not the case—not at all. Funds have a significant upside. The easy diversification within a market sector is a benefit that shouldn't be underestimated. Mutual funds are the choice for a lot of reasonable people. Furthermore, a lot of the people reading this book wouldn't be able to get away from mutual funds if they wanted to. Their 401(k)s will give a limited number of choices—and most, if not all, will be mutual funds.

Mutual funds will almost certainly be part of your retirement investment portfolio. You need to make the most of your mutual fund decisions so you don't get fleeced.

Selecting a Stock Fund

A variety of factors go into finding a good stock fund. Remember, there are thousands of funds out there, and depending on where you buy your funds, you may be pushed in one direction or another. Often you'll be steered toward funds that do the seller of the fund a lot of good, but aren't a great fit for you. Does your broker get a particularly sweet commission when he sells a certain fund? The following pages give a rundown of some of the most common factors that go into selecting a good fund.

WAXIE'S SIDEBAR: The Select List

Charles Schwab and Company is a discount brokerage. They offer low-priced services, like stock trades and mutual fund purchases for $9.95 a pop (which ain't so cheap; check my Web site to see who we recommend currently, it's cheaper! http://www.trendfund.com). They're also a mutual fund supermarket. You can select from Schwab's own funds or opt for a fund from T. Rowe Price, Vanguard, Fidelity, or a bunch of other sources—there are literally thousands of funds you can buy and sell through your Schwab account.

When you go through Schwab's mutual funds pages, you'll see a prominent mention of its Select List. The Select List funds are no-load, no-commission purchases. Schwab, on its Web site, www.schwab .com, gives a variety of criteria that are used in selecting the funds. I like Schwab, and, all in all, you could do lot worse than the funds in the Select List. But could you do better?

Sure, you can. I did some research and found several occasions where Schwab had a fund on its Select List that was very similar to another fund that could be purchased through Schwab but was not on the list. The fund on the Select List had no transaction cost at all; the other fund had a $50 purchase fee. So why pay the fee? Well, the management fee on the fund outside the list was a couple of tenths of a percentage point lower. The $50 would pay for itself almost instantly. And if I didn't want to pay the $50, I could simply open an account at a brokerage firm that created the other funds. (Note that the $50 could be excessive if you're planning on making frequently, regular contributions. If that's the case you should open up an account with the issuing fund's brokerage.)

I'm not trying to pick on Schwab here. It's a good company with good services. I just use this as an example of the strategies that can be used to steer you toward an investment that is less than optimal.

Stock Fund Categories

Most funds specialize in a specific sector of the market. Some funds concentrate on small companies, others on behemoths. Some funds hold bonds, others stocks. Some invest domestically, others internationally. Different international funds invest in different parts of the world.

Morningstar, which is the world's premier fund-rating firm (and which we'll talk about in more detail later) lists over sixty fund categories. It's confusing at first, but still, it's worth sticking with the Morningstar classifications. They're what you'll encounter most frequently; so using Morningstar's classification will allow you to speak the same language as your broker, the media, and the investment world in general.

At first it can be dizzying to try to keep track of so many different categories. But once you start breaking it down, you'll see that it's not that overwhelming.

Domestic Equity (Stocks)

Morningstar uses a matrix (also called a grid or style box) to identify how funds that invest in U.S stocks should be classified. Figure 10-1 (on page 133) uses the Morningstar matrix:

Each cell in the matrix represents a different category, creating nine in total: large value, large blend, large growth, mid value, mid blend, mid growth, small value, small blend, and small growth. What does it all mean? We'll start by looking at the columns in the table: value, growth, and blend.

These are measures of how quickly companies are expected to grow. A *value* investment holds shares in a company that is expected to be pretty stable, without potential huge returns. The shares of a value stock are moderately priced, and the companies are more likely to pay dividends.

A *growth* investment, however, is one that could achieve bigger returns. These companies spend more on expanding, and are more likely to reinvest their profits rather than pay dividends. Their shares are higher priced when compared to the company's returns. A *blend* fund holds a mix of value and growth stocks. Blend funds try to reflect the market for that size company as a whole.

The rows in the table refer to the size of the companies in the fund. Morningstar categorized every publicly traded company by its capitalization. Those in the top 72 percent are classified as *large*; those in the next 18 percent are said to be *mid*; and the final 10 percent are *small*.

Foreign Stocks

The world's a big place, so it shouldn't be surprising that there is a huge variety of fund categories for foreign funds. For starters, there's a matrix that's similar to the one given for domestic stock funds. The difference is that small and mid-sized companies are combined. So there are a total of six major categories: foreign large growth, foreign large blend, foreign large value, foreign small/mid growth, foreign small/mid blend, foreign small/mid value.

Then there are any number of available funds that invest in specific geographic regions. Morningstar recognizes the following geographic categories:

> *Latin America stock*
> *Europe stock*
> *Japan stock*
> *Pacific/Asia ex Japan (no Japanese stocks permitted)*
> *Diversified Pacific (all of Asia and Pacific, including Japan)*
> *World stock*

A geographic fund might include a mix of company sizes and growth potential.

Sector Categories

Many funds invest in specific market sectors. If you happen to feel that technology or health-care-related stocks are poised for a big run, you'd do well to invest in a sector-specific fund. Morningstar lists the following sector categories, among others:

Communications
Health
Natural resources
Precious metals
Real estate
Technologies
Utilities

WAXIE'S SIDEBAR:
Criticisms of Morningstar's Categories

In early July 2007, Chuck Jaffe of marketwatch.com reported that fund managers who attended a Morningstar conference expressed their displeasure with the Morningstar grid. Jaffe wrote: "The problem is that the financial advisory community has turned the boxes into straitjackets for money managers. They want a fund confined to a certain box, so that the advisor can build a portfolio certain in the knowledge that the fund represents a certain geography. When a manager moves from one box to the next, some investors bail out, fearing style drift.

"For investors, the offshoot is simple: Decide if you want funds that are rigid in what they do, or that have some flexibility. When the mutual fund industry started—and it was about 60 years before there was a Morningstar—funds were built to give professional management and diversification at a reasonable price.

"If you don't want management that is limited in how it acts, pick funds that have the ability to go anywhere or simply ride along with the manager when they tilt the fund a bit towards a certain style or cap size."

But you'd better really have confidence in a fund's managers before you opt for a fund that can pick any stock at any time.

Active Fund Management

Most funds have real, live people investing funds for you. These are known as *actively managed* funds. These folks have varying styles and abilities. Some are short; some are tall; some are risk averse; others prefer to gamble. As a group, they're a hoot. Invite all the fund managers you can over for dinner; you can hear about their Paris vacations or their daughter's debutant ball gowns. Or don't. I wouldn't, no shot. If you really want to learn any more about a particular fund manager's experience, you can look at the fund's prospectus or check out the Web site. You'll find a bio that lists experience, education, and notable accomplishments.

While all that biographical information may be charming, there's really one thing an investor wants to know about a fund manager: Is this guy or gal worth the money he or she's being paid. There are two benchmarks you can use to judge the quality of a fund's management. The first is quality of the fund's returns against those of its peers. When making this comparison it's important to compare funds that are similar to each other. There's nothing useful to be gained from comparing a domestic large value fund against a foreign small/mid growth fund. You'd expect the former to deliver predictable and not eye-popping returns. It's a relatively safe, stable investment.

In contrast, you'd expect some pretty wild swings out of small-cap foreign stocks. You might see some fabulous growth over a quarter or two and then a nasty dip soon after that. Over a short period, say twelve months, a small foreign stock fund might dazzle you with its returns. Or it might horrify you. This sector of the market is risky and you know it, or you should.

When comparing fund managers, you need to make sure you're comparing one against another in the same sector. It's only fair.

There is a second comparison you should make—and this one's really important. Just about every fund can be measured against some sort of index. Take a large blend fund, for example. A large blend fund invests in a variety of very large companies with a mix of growth potential. If you wanted to find a good list of funds that fit this description, you wouldn't have to look any further than the S&P 500. The S&P 500 is pretty much an objective list—it's the 500 largest companies, as measured by Standard and Poor's—and within the random sample you're bound to find companies with a big variety of growth objectives.

It is appropriate—and in fact, necessary—to compare the fund you're investing in against an appropriate index. There are dozens of indexes out there. For every market sector you can think of, there's an index. The most commonly used indexes are maintained by S&P and Russell. Check out the following Web pages to familiarize yourself with indexes and how they're performing.

- *Russell indexes:* http://www.russell.com/indexes/performance/default.asp
- *S&P:* http://www2.standardandpoors.com/spf/html/products/url_sandp_indices.htm

When you finally get involved in these sorts of comparisons, you're likely to make a plain discovery. While one manager may outperform another in the same sector over a year or two or five, that same manager is unlikely to have done a whole lot better than the index that he or she should be measured against. This is a nearly universal truth in the mutual fund world: Managers rarely outperform their underlying indexes. This leads one to an interesting question: Why do we pay these guys at all? The answer: We don't have to.

WAXIE'S TIP

If you want to keep some managed funds in your portfolio, make your purchases where they're likely to do the most good. An actively managed large-cap domestic value fund is, by its nature, made up of stocks that are known to about everyone. Really, will one fund manager have that much of a better feel of how GE is likely to do than some other manager. But in the smaller, more unpredictable sectors, a manager's skills may be more useful. In, for example, the small-cap Asia market, you may find a manager who really knows his or her stuff and has some picks that others haven't discovered.

Passive Fund Management

Passively managed funds do away with the high-priced managers who invest your money in the more common actively managed funds. Instead, these funds buy a few computers and program them to buy and sell shares that the funds mimic in a particular index. These funds are usually referred to as index funds. So how much can you save by investing in an index fund? As with everything else in the financial world, it depends. But if you choose correctly, the savings can be extraordinary. Take the Vanguard 500 Index Fund as an example. It's a large blend fund that pretty much mimics the S&P 500. It's management fee: 0.18 percent. What about those other costs? The Vanguard 500 comes with no loads, no redemption fees, and no 12b-1 fees.

Other Vanguard funds have similarly small fees; most are around 0.25 percent.

. . . .
WAXIE'S TIP

There are a number of good fund companies out there. But if you want to save yourself the trouble of going to dozens of companies to see every possible

available fund, you'd do well to start your fund searches with three companies: Vanguard, Fidelity, and T. Rowe Price. The funds of these companies
generally have very low fees. But, of course, look at the specifics of any fund
before investing.

Fees Revisited

I won't beat the dead horse much longer here. I think you get the
point I've made over and over: Fees will kill you, and you need to be
aware of exactly what you're paying for the sake of owning a fund.
There's no reason to ever pay loads. There are tons of good no-load
funds. Under no circumstances should you pay a management fee of
more than 1.5 percent. Even that's too high. Usually, if you're looking at a fund with a 1.5 management fee, you'll be able to find something that's very similar, and will deliver nearly identical returns, with
a smaller fee. The only time you might consider paying a fee that's as
high as 1.5 is if you find a managed fund that you believe can really
kick ass.

Most often, you'll be better off sticking to index funds. But even
if you hold mostly passively managed funds, you need to be diligent. I was doing some research recently and found a fund that was
nearly identical to the Vanguard S&P 500. The only real difference
between the two was that this second fund charged a 0.49 percent
management fee, as opposed to the Vanguard's 0.18. That small
number may seem trivial, but if you stop and look at the numbers,
you'll think differently. Table 10-1 shows just how much money
you'd be giving away with a single $25,000 fund purchase over a
thirty-year period, assuming the fund would grow at 9 percent per
year.

That would be $42,000 you'd be throwing away while getting no
benefit whatsoever. None.

TABLE 10-1. EFFECT OF MANAGEMENT FEES ON A $25,000 INVESTMENT OVER 30 YEARS

YEARS IN FUND	0.53 PERCENT FEE	0.18 PERCENT FEE
5	$ 37,539.48	$ 38,026.34
10	$ 56,368.49	$ 58,026.74
15	$ 84,641.75	$ 88,546.57
20	$ 127,096.27	$ 135,118.67
25	$ 190,845.10	$ 206,185.90
30	$ 286,569.00	$ 314,631.77

Fund Analysis

In these days of instant information and ubiquitous media, there are tons of outlets where you can educate yourself on mutual funds. If you have an online broker, you'll almost certainly have a variety of tools that allow you to look at a fund's vital information. Beyond the broker, there are some other good, unbiased sources you can turn to. For starters, let's say you want to learn about a particular fund. Maybe it's a fund that's already in your portfolio, or maybe it's one that's being offered by your 401(k) plan. How are you going to learn all you need to know about the fund?

Actually, you can turn to two of the most common references in the world: Google and Yahoo! They both maintain very solid finance sections at http://finance.google.com and http://finance.yahoo.com where you can easily learn most of what you'll need to know about any particular fund. Here's what you can expect to see if you type in the ticker symbol for a fund at Google Finance. The page will show the fund's sector as well as key financial data: rates of return, expense ratios, and a chart. Further down the page, you'll be able to learn about a fund's holdings and its availability through brokerages.

Yahoo! Finance isn't as immediate in its delivery of information, but it can be more thorough, giving easy links to research reports and mentions in major media. The Performance page on any fund gives important information about returns.

By browsing through these pages, you should get a pretty good idea of whether or not a fund is even worth considering. If the fees are too high or the fund has underperformed its market sector or peers, you can probably move on without giving it a whole lot of consideration. Make sure to look beyond the initial returns and look at how the fund has performed over the last five to ten years. Also look at the stability of its management. For index funds this isn't especially important, but for a managed fund, you want to know that the same management team that has done well in the past is likely to be there for a time. Tax information is also very important.

Once you get beyond the information available at Yahoo! and Google, you can turn back to Morningstar. We've already talked about Morningstar's categories. Without question, Morningstar is the most important fund-rating service in the world. They're pretty good at what they do. They give plenty of solid factual information, and their analysts' reports and ratings of mutual funds are widely respected. For many of the major funds on the market, some 2,000, they've amassed impressively thorough research.

No matter where you go to research funds, you're bound to see Morningstar's star ranking system. Every fund gets a number of stars, from one to five, and many funds crow loudly about the number of stars Morningstar has bestowed upon them. This is useful information, but hardly the only thing you need to know about a fund.

To create its star ranking, Morningstar compares all of the funds in a given sector. It looks at the returns over one, five, and ten years. Then it evaluates the fees and the risk a fund has taken on to achieve its gains. Those who have taken more risk are more likely to get a lower ranking. The funds in the top 10 percent of their category get five stars; the next 22.5 percent get four stars; the following 35 percent three stars. The last 22.5 percent and bottom 10 percent get two stars and one star respectively.

The system is objective and fair, and you could do a lot worse than just picking funds with high Morningstar ratings. But you're best off using Morningstar's star ratings as a starting point for your searches. Remember the stars only look at the fund's history. To get a fuller view of a fund's future potential, you need to look at the full Morningstar reports, which include a lot of detailed mathematical analysis as well as an analyst's view of the fund. These reports are excellent and well worth looking at before you buy a fund.

You can get access to Morningstar from a few sources:

■ *Brokerages.* Usually brokerages sell Morningstar reports for $10 or $15 a shot. Some even give them for free. At the time of this writing, just for creating an online account at T. Rowe Price, with no deposit necessary, you'd get access to Morningstar reports. (https://www3.troweprice.com/aaweb1/accountAccess/publicBen efitsOfRegistration.do)

■ *Morningstar site.* Morningstar has free reports that are available on the site. In addition, they have a premium service that may very well be worth the $145 per year fee. The premium has a very nice screening look that I'll discuss later.

■ *Your library.* Morningstar puts out *500 Funds* every year, a book that details the best mutual funds they've seen. Get it for free with your library card.

Fund Screeners

Both Yahoo! and Google have nifty tools called Fund Screeners. There are online applications that allow you to enter all the criteria that you'd like to use in judging a fund. For example, you can choose a fund category, the longevity of management, and dollar value of the fund. The Morningstar screener has some prebuilt screens that lead you toward excellent funds in different sectors. These are excellent tools. Be sure to use them.

WAXIE'S SIDEBAR: Unconventional Funds

The government has put restrictions on what you can do in your IRA accounts. You can't day-trade, you can't sell short, and you can't make full use of options. Your banking institution may put additional restrictions on what you can do with your money. There's actually a logic to the restrictions. The government created tax-friendly IRAs with two basic goals in mind: encouraging savings and encouraging long-term investment. Neither of these goals would be met if we could do some naked-option straddling in our IRAs.

Despite these restrictions, there are a couple of ways to play short-term trends in the markets in your IRAs. Rydex, a mutual fund and ETF company, has created a group of "Dynamic" funds with some interesting goals. The S&P 500 2x fund, for example, attempts to replicate the daily movements in the S&P 500 times 2. So if the S&P jumps 2 percent in a day, the fund sees a 4 percent increase. As you might imagine, a fund like this will create some serious swings. The fund saw a 34 percent decline in 2001 and a 46 percent decline in 2002. In 2003, however, the fund managed a 56 percent gain. If you're feeling bearish about the market, you could invest in the Inverse S&P 500 2x which returns double the negative returns of the S&P 500.

Rydex has dynamic funds for a variety of indexes, including the Dow Jones Industrial Average, the Nasdaq 100, and the Russell 2000. See the Rydex Web site for a full listing: http://www.rydexfunds.com/our products/fund_profiles.shtml.

These funds are far more dangerous than other funds. Rydex uses extremely complex financial instruments to achieve these results, which introduces types of risk that you won't get with other funds. These are not good instruments for typical buy-and-hold investors. Make sure you look at these funds closely—read the prospectus—before putting any money into them.

Exchange-Traded Funds

A few years ago a new investment vehicle came on the scene, an exchange-traded fund. ETFs have generated a fair amount of excitement. Today, they're everywhere. Even if you're new to the term ETF, you've probably heard of some of the bigger ones—Spiders (SPDRs) and Cubes (QQQQ), which advertise frequently on television during golf tournaments and other sporting events.

I'm discussing ETFs here because they are quite similar to mutual funds in a lot of respects. An ETF, like a mutual fund, is a collection of stocks. Like an index mutual fund, an ETF is managed by computers with the goal of mimicking some underlying index, such as the S&P 500 or the Wilshire 5000. In fact, an ETF serves many of the same purposes as a mutual fund, and as you'll see, under some circumstances you'd do well to forgo a mutual fund in order to buy an ETF.

To help you understand what ETFs are exactly, I'm going to start by highlighting the differences.

The Birthing of Mutual Funds and ETFs

A mutual fund gets off the ground when some investment company decides it can pull together enough money. With a sizable amount of cash in hand, the fund starts buying stocks. The value of the stocks along with any cash is calculated, the liabilities are determined, and the fund is priced accordingly. This calculation determines what's known as the net asset value, or NAV. Once the mutual fund is made available to investors, the NAV is recalculated every day after the closing of the market. All buy and sell orders are executed at that time at the day's NAV price. When you buy into a fund or sell your way out of it, your transaction occurs with the fund's owners and managers. For instance, when you sell a fund, the fund needs to pass cash your way. Then the fund must adjust its portfolio to reflect the changes in the amount it has under management.

An ETF has a different start. Rather than rising from a pool of cash supplied by investors, an ETF starts with a pile of stock that is borrowed from a variety of sources (usually pension funds and large investment houses). The exact contents of the pool of stock are constantly managed so that the value of the pool closely mimics the corresponding index on a moment-by-moment basis. Shares in the ETF are then traded on the market, just like stocks. Unlike mutual funds, transactions don't wait till the end of the day; they're executed whenever buyers and sellers come together at an agreed-upon price.

The fact that ETFs are traded in this manner makes them very dynamic investments. A savvy investor like myself can do all sorts of things with an ETF that I couldn't possibly do with a mutual fund. For starters, I can put limit or stop orders on trades. I can sell short. I can even buy and sell options on ETFs.

● ●

WAXIE'S NOTE

There is a technical matter that's worth keeping in mind as you deal with ETFs. A share in a mutual fund has its price set by determining its net asset value at the close of a trading day. But for an ETF, market forces determine the price of a share. As the market price fluctuates in an ETF, the NAV may go a bit higher or lower than the market price. Because there are very savvy people looking to make money through arbitrage on any gaps that do occur, the gap never gets too big. So the gap between the NAV and the actual price shouldn't concern you much.

● ●

Advantages of ETFs

One of the greatest attributes of ETFs is that they have absolutely tiny management fees. Some have expense fees of less than 0.1 percent, and they rarely get higher than 0.25 percent, which is better than many (i.e., most) index mutual funds. Even if you found an index fund with a rock-bottom management fee, you might not be able to get into it. Take the Fidelity Spartan 500 Index Fund, for example. It's a great fund. Matched to the S&P 500, it has a tiny expense ratio of 0.1 percent. The only potential problem is that the minimum investment is $10,000. If you don't have that kind of cash, however, you can buy into the same index by investing in an ETF. SPDRs (SPY) and iShares S&P 500 Index (IVV) both cover the S&P 500 and have expense ratios of about 0.08-0.09 percent. You can buy as much of it as your budget will handle—a few bucks or hundreds of thousands.

ETFs are also pretty tax-efficient. Usually, ETFs don't accumulate capital gains, which could help if you're holding the ETF outside of a retirement account.

Another big selling point of ETFs is that there is an ETF covering nearly every tiny segment of the market you can think of. Say that through your work or your interests, you have a keen knowledge of some small portion of the market, whether it be biotech or retail or home building. Should you have a real sense that your sector is going to move in some substantial way, you could buy or sell short through an ETF without having to place a bet on any individual company that might or might not react the way the sector as a whole would. There are also ETFs for nearly every other world market I can think of, and then some. Same goes for currency.

There are mega ETFs. You want to buy something you can't find? Check on-line to see if there is a corresponding ETF. You may be surprised and find it available in ETF form.

Drawbacks of ETFs

Sounds pretty good, right? Well, they are. But that's not to say that you should dump all your mutual funds in favor of ETFs. The major disadvantage of ETFs is that they generate all the fees you get with a stock transaction. This may or may not be a big deal, depending on how you're planning on buying into an ETF. If you're planning on making a one lump-sum purchase for a significant sum of money, then an ETF is just fine, especially if you're with a discount broker who charges $5 or $10 a trade. If, however, you're planning on making frequent purchases, perhaps through some retirement savings plan, then the fees can really add up, especially when compared to a similar index mutual fund that comes with no loads or transactions fees.

The other main drawback for potential ETF investors is the treatment of dividends. In a mutual fund you can choose to have your dividends automatically reinvested in the fund. That way, you don't have to think about what happens with the cash that flows out of the fund. It's a nice way to ensure that you're compounding your investments. But with ETFs, dividends and any other cash disbursements get deposited in your account. Want to reinvest it in the ETF? You'll incur a transaction fee.

But perhaps the biggest downside of ETFs is that many are not well thought out and organized, particularly those covering a small market sector. Some of these ETFs, which claim to be following a particular index (or just an industry), haven't diversified themselves properly. Before you buy any ETF, you need to do your research;

look at Google Finance, Yahoo! Finance, and Morningstar to see if you think the fund is well run.

To sum up, ETFs will work best under the following conditions:

■ *You wish to trade on the indexes more actively or with more sophistication than is possible with a mutual fund.*

■ *You're making large lump-sum purchases rather than small incremental purchases.*

■ *You're buying outside of a 401(k) or IRA and would like the tax advantage that comes with ETFs.*

■ *You want to buy a fund based on a thin market sector.*

In most typical retirement investing situations, when you're making regular investments through a 401(k), a good index fund is probably the better vehicle.

Sector Superstars

To close out this section, I wanted to give some final advice that I hope will set you on the path to choosing the right funds. Whatever you do, you're going to want to spend a good chunk of time shopping for funds. You'd better, because it's all a part of learning to Rule Your Freakin' Retirement! Your choices in funds and fund sectors will have to fit your goals for risk, growth, and diversification. We'll talk more about these factors when we discuss allocation later. Even now, you probably get the idea that each of the sectors you invest in and each of the funds you choose will serve a specific purpose.

A Large Blend Blaster

A large blend fund will usually give you a broad section of stocks that probably won't set the world on fire, but will give you some nice and reasonable steady growth over time. In fact, looking at the S&P 500 over the last ten years, you can see some very nice returns.

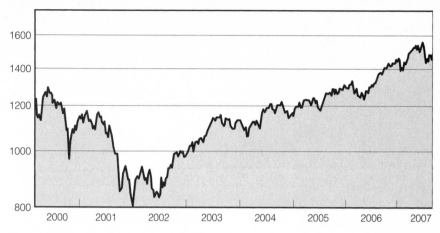

Figure 10.2   S&P 500 since 2000

If you bought into an S&P index in 2002, you would be a very happy camper right about now. If you bought in earlier than 2001, you'd have had some rough years, but still come out okay by 2007.

You need to understand that buying into a fund that fits Morningstar's large blend category doesn't mean you're getting a fund that serves remotely the same purpose as an S&P index fund.

To prove the point, take a look at the Janus Contrarian fund (see Figure 10.3). It gets five stars from Morningstar and fits into the large blend section of the matrix. There's no doubt, that by Morningstar's criteria, this fund deserves five stars. Hell, if they had a sixth, they should hand that over, too. It's totally been kicking the index's ass. Outpacing it in an absolutely devastating way, while still keeping management fees pretty reasonable. That's what I call a double ka-chingo!

So you should run out and snatch this one up, right? I mean, why put money in an index fund when you can get these sorts of returns while still fulfilling your portfolio's needs? As you've probably guessed, the Janus Contrarian doesn't invest in the same sort of stocks as what you might initially think. You have to dig into the literature a little bit, but once you do, you'll see that 40 percent of the

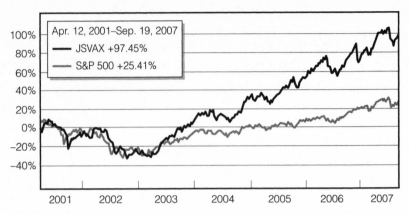

Figure 10.3 JSVAX vs. S&P 500

fund's holdings are international. And some of them seem pretty eccentric. Heck, one of its top holdings is Tenega Nasional. Never heard of it? Shocking! It's the largest electrical utility in Malaysia. And trust me, it's not part of the S&P 500.

There's nothing wrong with Janus Contrarian. Not at all. It has performed spectacularly. I just want to point out that when you're buying into *any* fund, you need to know exactly what you're getting into. If you want a Malaysian utility in your large blend lineup, cool. If not, look on and look out.

Foreign Large Growth Grumbler

Most of us are looking to put at least some portion of our portfolio into funds that have serious potential. Sure, slow and steady wins the race, but wouldn't you like to have a winning sprinter in there as well. The foreign market funds are generally where you're going to find the funds with the potential to do some serious damage.

One of the funds in this category, the William Blair Growth Fund, once saw a 42 percent spike *in three months*. Of course, this sort of return isn't typical, and with foreign stocks, especially ones with smaller capitalizations, you can expect some serious ups and downs.

The following chart shows two years' worth of returns for the William Blair fund and the index against which it should be judged. Of course, there are index funds and ETFs that cover this sector, and the William Blair fund's expenses are rather high.

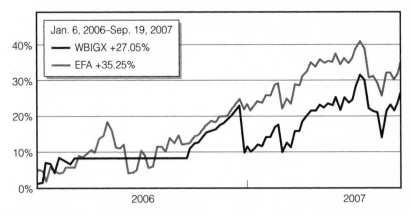

Figure 10.4   WBIGX vs. EFA

Again it's a matter of the proper foreknowledge of expectation and risk. When you're looking, you might see some funds with some crazy high returns. But they'll have taken on a lot of risk to get that sort of payout, and you need to be ready for the really, really bad days should they occur (when they occur).

Mid-Cap Madness

Domestic mid-cap stocks should give you some of the pizzazz and excitement that comes with a lot of growth potential, but the craziness is tempered by the stability that comes with domestic holdings. There are a couple of indexes in this sector, the S&P 400 MidCap being a common choice. Like most everything else, these stocks got absolutely hammered in 2001 and 2002. You can see what the declines looked like in Figure 10.5.

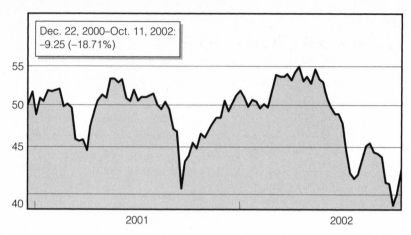

Figure 10.5 S&P 400 MidCap Fund 2001–02

I know I've said it before, but you need to keep in mind that these sorts of setbacks are not only entirely possible, they are inevitable. Nothing goes *up,* or *down,* in a straight line. When they come, you need to be ready for them. But as you can see in Figure 10.6, the index has rebounded well since then. (Until 2008's debacle.)

These are just a few of the sectors you can invest in. Before you put your hard-earned money into any sector or fund, make sure you have a good understanding of what you're getting yourself into.

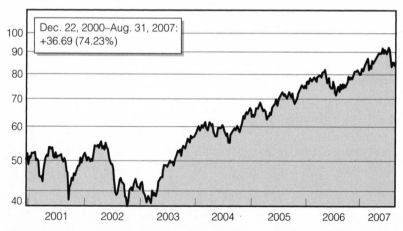

Figure 10.6 S&P 400 MidCap Fund 2001–07

Quiz

1. **What does a 12b-1 fee cover?**

   a. Management fees

   b. Marketing fees

   c. All fees

   Answer: b

2. **A passively managed fund is also known as:**

   a. An ETF

   b. A small-cap fund

   c. A value fund

   d. An index fund

   Answer: d

3. **When do mutual fund purchases and sales take place?**

   a. At close of a trading day

   b. Before the start of a trading day

   c. Throughout the trading day

   Answer: a

4. **When do ETF purchases and sales take place?**

   a. At close of a trading day

   b. Before the start of a trading day

   c. Throughout the trading day

   Answer: c

Chapter 11

Bonds and Bond Funds

I'm a stock market guy, well, maybe not a "stock" guy, but a stock trader dude, okay? There, I said it. I said it and I'm okay with it, wowsa! I made millions trading stocks and options, making money off of trends I learned to recognize and exploit. As closely as I've been watching the stock markets for the last several years, I've seen some crazy things. I was around for the tech bubble in the late nineties and the bursting of the bubble that followed. I know a lot of people—good, smart people—who got killed when the bubble burst. They made the mistake that so many did in those days, or in any bubble market: They came to believe that stocks are the be-all and end-all of investing. They wanted the huge returns that stocks seemed to offer, so they invested everything they had in tech and Internet stocks. It was a disastrous decision. Some lost so much when the markets crashed that they had to put off retirement. I know people who had to work for years longer then they had planned because they were too reliant on stocks.

Don't make the same mistake yourself. You need diversity in your financial portfolio. And bonds are an extremely important part of a well-rounded portfolio.

· · · · · · · · · · · · · · · · · · ·
WAXIE'S TIP

A market is a market for a reason; you can and should make money no matter which way prices go. *Nothing* goes up in a straight line, and nothing beyond nothing goes up forever. What's the old saying? "The bigger the bubble, the louder the—*pop!*"

Bond Basics

What's a bond? It's pretty simple, really. Imagine that your state government wants to start a highway construction project, but the politicians have no desire to raise taxes. To get the cash the state needs to build the roadway, the state can put itself into debt. Essentially, the state puts out a piece of paper that says, if you buy this paper—this IOU—the state will pay you back with a defined rate of interest over a specific period of time. So you buy the bond, the state eventually builds the road, and over the life of the bond, you get periodic interest payments. At the end of the life of the bond, you get back the principal, the amount of your original investment.

Debts by way of bonds are extremely common and are offered by a variety of entities—local, state, and federal governments, as well as corporations.

The return on a bond—the amount the holder makes in interest—is determined by the risk associated with a given bond. For example, a bond sold by the U.S. government pays a relatively low rate of interest. This makes sense, as it's exceedingly unlikely that the U.S. government is going to go bankrupt and default on its debt obligations. Anything is possible, but if that does happen, then there's a lot more to worry about than whether or not your bonds aren't worth much. On the other hand, a small company that's been battered by fraud and accounting scandals will have to pay a very high rate of return on the bonds because there's a pretty decent chance the company will go belly-up and the bonds will become worthless. You may have heard of Michael Milken who made billions trading in these so-called junk bonds. These are bonds that are high risk, non-investment grade bonds. Bonds get graded based on their safety and stability. Junk bonds are often considered BB or less. Any A bonds are just that—Grade-A—and considered safe and not junk. Later in this chapter you'll learn more about the rating system.

....
WAXIE'S TIP

In 2008 this rating system was integral to the ups and downs of the stock market. Seemingly every time one of the key mortgage lenders rating went down, the market tanked, and every time the rating was affirmed (not many were raised!) the market would rally. These ratings do carry a lot of weight for investors and lenders, so you should pay attention to them. Bear Stearns's ratings slipped and the smart money bet Bear Stearns was gonna go under, and they certainly did go under, making those people who paid attention a *lot* of money. And it left a lot of investors, some very savvy billionaires with big reputations, holding the proverbial bag! Pay attention if a bond you are holding gets its rating slashed. It very well may be time to sell, sell—*SELL!*

Buying Bonds

When you buy a bond, you don't have to hold it and collect the interest; you can buy and sell bonds on the open market just as you would a stock. The same brokerages that handle transactions of stocks, mutual funds, and ETFs will also handle the trading of bonds. Furthermore, there are groupings of bonds—bond funds—that work very much like the stock funds I discussed in the previous chapter.

You'll learn more about risk, bond types, and bond funds and much more as this chapter continues. But first you need to understand some of the vocabulary that comes with bonds. Before I give you the definitions, I'll give a quick warning: When people talk about bonds, their language quickly gets jargon-heavy. There's really no way around it. To accurately assess a bond, you need to judge it on specific, technical criteria, and if you don't get the words exactly right, you may not understand the true nature of the bond you're considering purchasing, and that's never a good idea.

The Language of Bonds

Maturity Date and Par Value

Bonds gather interest for a given period of time—as little as seven days, as long as thirty years. At the end of that period of time, the original amount paid for the bond is returned to the bondholder. The date at which the original investment is returned is known as the *maturity date*. The amount that will be returned to the bondholder is known as the *par value*. If you were to buy a ten-year $1,000 bond directly from the U.S. Treasury on May first of 2009, you'd expect the bond to *mature* in May of 2019, at which time you'd get your *par value* of $1,000 back.

Coupon Rate

Bonds offer a known rate of return. For example, you may buy a corporate bond for $1,000, knowing that it will return 5 percent a year. Every year until the maturity date, the bond owner can expect $50. This percentage is called the *coupon rate*. Keep in mind that the coupon rate refers to the percentage of interest received on the par value of the bond.

The Problem With Relying on Par Value and Coupon Rate

As I mentioned before, bonds are bought and sold on the market, and there's no saying that you're going to be buying your bond from the issuing entity. You may buy a bond on the market at a price that is above or below that of par value.

Why would the price be higher or lower than the issuing price, or par value? Bond prices change because interest rates change. When interest rates go up, bond issuers have to raise their rate of return accordingly; when rates go down, bond rates also move down. These fluctuations have a direct impact on the price of bonds in the markets. The following example will illustrate why this is the case.

Let's just say you buy a five-year, $1,000 corporate bond with a 5 percent coupon rate. (That is, the bond will give you $50 a year until the maturity date, at which time you get the $1,000 par value back.) The day after you purchase this bond, interest rates go up drastically and the return on newer bonds goes up to 7.5 percent. (This sort of jump would never happen, but it makes for a good example.) If at that time you decide that you want to sell your $1,000 5 percent bond on the market, you'll have a problem: Nobody is going to want to buy a $1,000 bond that pays 5 percent when they can get one that pays 7.5 percent. Would you? No freakin' way, dude, right? So, the question is: How can you compensate? You can't change the interest rate the bond pays: That's fixed. All you can do, if you want to get rid of the bond, is lower the purchase price so that the overall rate is competitive with the new issue.

Note that the farther a bond is from its maturity date, the more the price of the bond will be affected by changes in the interest rate. When you think about it, this makes perfect sense. The longer the bond is from maturity the longer you'll be stuck with the coupon rate. If rates go up, you could have a bond with a relatively bad rate for a long time. It's going to be harder to unload that bond, so the price will be pretty low. You'll hear more about how the remaining life of a bond is measured in the upcoming sections.

Yield

Those looking to buy bonds on the secondary market and exchange, are not so concerned with the coupon rate (the rate relative to the par value). They're more concerned with the rate relative to the actual price they're paying. In the bond world, the rate as measured against the price paid on the secondary market is known as the *yield*. A simple mathematical formula will give you the yield of a bond: You divide the amount of return over the course of the year by the actual purchase price.

Now look again at the unfortunate bond purchase I just discussed. You bought a $1,000 bond at 5 percent only to see the movements in interest rate push the market return rate to 7.5 percent. What are you going to have to do to the price of your 5 percent bond to give it the same yield? You'd have to lower the price drastically, to right around $650 ($650×0.075=$48.75).

On the secondary bond market, yield is a better measure of a bond's return than coupon rate. There are some other measures that are more accurate still.

Yield to Maturity

Another key measure of a bond's value is its *yield to maturity*. A yield to maturity calculation assumes that the bondholder will receive all the coupon payments, which will be reinvested in a bond at the same rate, and that the bondholder will keep the bond to the maturity date, at which time it will be redeemed for par value. When you factor the total amount of money gained over the remaining life of the bond, you get a pretty clear picture of your true rate of return on the actual purchase price. The sidebar (on page 167) that looks at an actual bond listing gives a good example of why yield to maturity is such a valuable measure.

Zero-Coupon Bonds

Most bonds make the periodic interest payments at the coupon rate. There is a type of bond, however, that disburses no money as the bond matures. With these bonds, you buy at a price lower than the par value. Then, as time goes by, the bond gains in value until its maturity date, which is when it can be redeemed for the full par value. For example, you may buy a $1,000 par value one-year zero-coupon bond. You pay only $960, or whatever the price is, for the sake of getting $1,000 in return on date of maturation.

Callable Bonds

With some bonds, the issuing agency reserves the right to redeem the bond before the maturity date, at which point it will stop making interest rates. Usually this involves the paying of some premium above the par value. Notice that in the sidebar (on page 167) that gives a bond listing, the bond is noncallable.

Bond Types

Bonds can be issued by federal, state, and local governments, as well as corporations.

Government Bonds

The federal government issues bonds to cover its (massive) debts through the Treasury Department's Bureau of Public Debt. When you go to your online broker, you'll see an entire section labeled "Treasuries." There are all sorts of Treasuries, with times to maturity ranging from a mere month to as long as thirty years. The names of the Treasuries differ with the length of time to maturity:

· · · · · · · · · · · · · · · · · ·
WAXIE'S TIP

Wanna buy bonds directly from the government? Head over to http://www.treasury direct.gov. All the government's current offerings can be purchased right there.

Treasury Bill

Also known as T-bills, Treasury bills mature in one year or less. Treasury bills don't pay a coupon rate. Rather, these are *zero-coupon bonds*. When you buy a T-bill, you pay less than the par value. You make your interest when it comes time to cash in your bond for full par value. For example, at the time I wrote this chapter, you could buy a three-month $1,000 T-bill for $987. At the end of the three-month period, you make your $13 when the government gives you $1,000.

Treasury Note

Treasury notes have maturity dates of two to ten years from their purchase date. They make coupon payments every six months.

Treasury Bonds

Treasury bonds are the longest-term Treasuries, lasting from ten to thirty years. They're sold quarterly.

WAXIE'S SIDEBAR: Examining a Bond Listing

Here's an actual listing for a bond I could have purchased through my broker as I wrote this chapter. I want to go through this listing so that you can see the key factors involved in a bond purchase.

U.S. TREASURY BOND 8.75% 5/17DUE 5/15/17

SECURITY DETAILS

Cusip:	912810DY1
Maturity Date:	5/15/2017
Coupon Rate %:	8.75
Coupon Type:	Fixed
Coupon Frequency:	Semi-Annual
Dated Date:	5/15/1987
First Coupon Date:	11/15/1987
Next Coupon Date:	11/15/2007
First Settle Date:	5/15/1987
Marginable:	—

OFFER

Price:	134.27343
Yield to Maturity %:	4.368

(continued)

U.S. TREASURY BOND 8.75% 5/17 DUE 5/15/17 (*continued*)

Yield to Call %:	—
Yield to Worst %:	—
Current Yield %:	6.517
Price Disclaimer:	Price based on 1 bond and a settlement date of 9/11/2007

CALL/SINK/PUT FEATURES

Call Type:	Noncallable
Call Schedule:	—

U.S. TREASURY BOND 8.75% 5/17 DUE 5/15/17: Here we have the particulars of the bond. It pays 8.75 percent on a par value, which on this bond is $1,000. So the annual payment is $87.50.

CUSIP: Every bond has a unique alphanumeric code that identifies it.

DATE INFORMATION: The next few lines tell you when the bond was issued and when it's due. This bond was issued by the Treasury 5/15/1987. From the top of the listing we know it reaches maturity in 2017, so it is a thirty-year note. The bond pays interest (the coupon) of $87.50 in May and November every year.

PRICE: This was a $1,000 bond, but because the interest rate offered by the bond was greater than the interest rate at the time I wrote this, the bond is more expensive than the $1,000 par value. The price listing gives the percentage of the par value the bond is selling for, or $1,342. When fees and other factors are included, I'd expect to pay a little more.

CURRENT YIELD: You know this bond is going to pay $87.50 per year. You can determine the yield by dividing the coupon rate by the price. ($87.50÷$1,342=0.00651, or 6.5 percent).

YIELD TO MATURITY: You can't really calculate the yield to maturity on the fly. But it's easy to see that the yield to maturity is lower than the current yield. This is because, when the bond matures, you're only going to get back par value, which is substantially less than the amount you'd have to pay for this bond. Assuming that you're going to reinvest your coupon payments, the yield to maturity is the best measure of what the bond will pay over its lifetime.

Munis

States and localities also issue bonds. In New York alone, you can find bonds issued by the state government; state agencies like the Metropolitan Transit Authority, and various townships and cities. State and local governments are a little more vulnerable than the federal government; that is, they have a slightly higher chance of going bankrupt. For this reason, munis pay slightly higher interest rates than Treasuries. Municipal bonds often come with some tax advantages, which I'll talk about later in the chapter.

WAXIE'S SIDEBAR: Can a Government Go Bust?

Yup! Municipal bonds are very safe investments because most state and local governments will be around and functioning for a good long time. But it's worth remembering the case of Orange County before thinking of municipal bonds as risk-free. In 1994, Orange County, California, a wealthy bedroom community, filed for bankruptcy after some needlessly risky investments went bad. The county treasurer of Orange County used extremely complex financial instruments to place what was essentially an enormous bet on the stability of interest rates. The county, which had been profiting for years with this strategy, didn't ask the right questions. Many saw great returns and never stopped to ask how they were achieved. The government never put in place the safeguards to ensure that the money under the treasurer's control was invested with an appropriate level of risk.

It's hard to believe that what happened in Orange County can never happen again, or is unique. If you want to read more about the Orange County bankruptcy, there's a nice article on erisk.com: http://www.erisk .com/Learning/CaseStudies/OrangeCounty.asp.

Quasi-Government Agencies

The U.S. government has been in the business of encouraging home ownership for a while now. During the Great Depression, home prices crumbled and banks wanted nothing to do with home mortgages. President Franklin D. Roosevelt, as part of the New Deal, created the Federal National Mortgage Association (Fannie Mac) and the Federal Home Mortgage Corporation (Freddie Mac) to make mortgages easier to get. These are private corporations that are backed by "the full faith and credit" of the U.S. government.

Mortgages, of course, involve a lot of debt, and Fannie Mae and Freddie Mac package that debt and sell portions as bonds. These bonds usually pay a little more than Treasuries. In 2008, Fannie Mae and Freddie Mac basically went bust, and federal intervention was necessary to stabilize the system.

WAXIE'S SIDEBAR: Yet Another Bond Mess

In 2007, the financial markets were thrown into turmoil because of some of the dealings around mortgage-back securities. Fannie Mae and Freddie Mac did not float the securities that caused all the problems. Rather, banks and other lending institutions sold mortgages to people who were a huge credit risk. They rolled these mortgages into securities and sold them on the markets. Individuals and institutions bought these securities, thinking that the rate of return was favorable and the risk was minimal. Well, it turned out that the risk was greater than anyone thought. Huge numbers of families defaulted on mortgages they couldn't afford, and the bonds that packaged the debts became totally worthless. The repercussions of these defaults sent shockwaves through almost every sector of the global economy. Hopefully, this mess didn't personally affect you. But let the mortgage mess of 2007 and 2008 serve as a reminder that there's risk in all investments.

Corporations

Large corporations like General Electric and Pfizer will offer bonds to fund certain initiatives. These can pay higher rates than any other bond types. But that's because there's inherently more risk in taking on the debt of a corporation than there is in taking on the debt of a government. The shakier the company, the more the bond's going to pay.

Bonds and Taxes

When considering a bond or a bond fund, you need to consider its tax implications. Treasuries are taxed on the federal level, but not on the state or local level. Munis can be triple-tax-free (no state, federal, or local) if you buy a bond from the state in which you live. Corporate bonds have no special tax status.

So when you're looking at a listing of funds, you'll notice that munis will pay lower rates of return than Treasuries. They're factoring in the tax advantage. If you're in a lower tax bracket, a Treasury usually works out a little better than a muni; the reverse is true for those in high tax brackets. There's a simple formula for figuring the tax equivalency of bonds, but the easiest way to figure out what type of bond is best for your is to go to an online calculator. This one from Morningstar is straightforward and useful: http://screen.morningstar.com/ BondCalc/BondCalculator_TaxEquivalent.html.

Evaluating Bond Risk

The return on bonds is determined by the risk associated with it. A Treasury, therefore, is bound to pay less than a municipal bond offered by some flat-broke township. And large, stable corporations pay less for their debt than small, unstable ones. But there are a lot of corporations and municipalities out there and there's no way you, with a limited knowledge of a town's financial stability, could judge the worth of the bonds these entities could create. That's where Moody's and Standard and Poor's come in.

Moody's and S&P assign a grade to a bond associated with its risk. For Moody's, that highest bond rating is Aaa. From there the ratings go to Aa, A, Baa, Ba, B, Caa, Ca, and C. For S&P, the highest-rated bonds are AAA, followed by AA, A, BBB, BB, B, CCC, CC, C. You will also find plus and minus ratings for even greater subtlety. For example, a bond might be rated BBB+ or AA−. Sometimes when people talk about the ratings of a bond they'll say it's "prime" or "investment grade." Table 11-1 shows how Moody's and S&P's ratings translate to these other definitions.

TABLE 11-1. BOND RATINGS AND THEIR DEFINITIONS

MOODY'S RATING	S&P RATING	DEFINITION
Aaa	AAA	Prime
Aa1	AA+	High grade/High quality
Aa2	AA	High grade/High quality
Aa3	AA−	High grade/High quality
A1	A+	Upper-medium grade
A2	A	Upper-medium grade
A3	A−	Upper-medium grade
Baa1	BBB+	Lower-medium grade
Baa2	BBB	Lower-medium grade
Baa3	BBB−	Lower-medium grade
Ba1	BB+	Noninvestment grade
Ba2	BB	Speculative
Ba3	BB−	Speculative

MOODY'S RATING	S&P RATING	DEFINITION
B1	B+	Highly speculative
B2	B	Highly speculative
B3	B–	Highly speculative

Of course, the exact rates that a particular ratings grade will offer will vary, depending on the interest rates at the time. In case you're curious, at the time I wrote this chapter a municipal ten-year AAA bond offered a 3.56 yield, while an A bond offered a 3.79 yield. On the corporate side, a ten-year AAA bond offered 5.21 percent while an A bond offered 5.81 percent. Find the current bond rates at Yahoo! Finance: http://finance.yahoo.com/bonds/composite_bond_rates.

Bond Funds

Bonds are an excellent investment, but it's difficult to amass a decent selection of bonds on your own. Some bonds have minimum purchase prices of $25,000, so it can be hard to accumulate a good, diverse set of bonds. Even if you have hundreds of thousands to put into bonds, you'll have to do a lot of shopping to figure out the mix of bonds that's best for you. As you've probably guessed, those clever people at banks and investment houses have come up with an alternative. They've extended the concepts used in stock mutual funds to the bond world. You can buy into a fund where you and all the other investors will collectively own and share in the profits of dozens, or even hundreds, of bonds.

There are thousands of bond funds to choose from. Getting your head around the choices can be challenging. You need to start breaking the funds into categories. For starters, you need to know that bond funds usually concentrate on bonds with similar lengths to maturity. Generally, there are short-term funds, intermediate-term funds, and long-term funds. Though there aren't rock-solid definitions as to what differentiates the different categories, it's generally accepted that an intermediate-term fund concentrates on bonds with maturity dates of about five to ten years in the future. Short-term and long-term funds fall on either side of intermediate-term funds. Morningstar, the fund-rating service we talked about so extensively in the stock mutual fund chapter, created a matrix quite similar to the one I showed in the mutual fund chapter, that categorizes most bond funds:

Short	Int.	Long	
			High
			Med.
			Low

The columns in the matrix give the length to maturity, and thus the interest rate sensitivity, while the rows offer the ratings of the bonds held within the fund. The "High" column is for funds that invest only in bonds that have the top ratings by Moody's and Standard and Poor's.

Morningstar has other categories as well. For starters, Morningstar has separate categories for bonds that are composed fully of government bonds and those that mix government with other bonds. So, for example, Morningstar has separate categories for long-term government and plain long-term. Other Morningstar categories include:

- *Inflation-protected bond*
- *Multisector bond*
- *Ultrashort*
- *Emerging markets*
- *High yield*
- *Bank load*
- *Munis.* There are separate categories for a variety of municipalities.

How Bond Funds Make You Money

When you buy a bond outright, with the intention of holding it to maturity, you know exactly how you're going to make your money: You'll receive your coupon payments and then, at maturity, you'll get your investment back. But if the market's favorable, or if you just don't want to own the bond anymore, you might sell your bond on the secondary market. At that time it may be selling for more than par value, at which time your profit would be equal to the price you collected above par value plus the coupons you collected.

The same principles work for bond funds. The fund will collect coupons on the bonds it holds, and, in addition, the bonds themselves—the assets within the fund—may gain or lose value depending on what happens with interest rates. If all goes well in your bond-fund purchasing endeavors, you'll collect some interest (or reinvest your coupons in the fund), then sell your shares for a profit when the time is right.

Comparing Bond Funds

When shopping for bond funds, it's vital to compare bond funds to others having similar attributes. A short-term fund is bound to have lower coupon returns than a long-term fund, but a long-term fund is much more vulnerable to price fluctuations due to movements in interest rates. Even the large classifications offered by Morningstar aren't detailed enough to ensure that you're making good comparisons.

The Key Measure in Bond Funds: Duration

It should be clear at this point that the time remaining on a bond is a key measure of the bond's value. The farther a bond is from maturity, the more vulnerable it is to changes in interest rate. So far in this chapter we've talked about a couple of ways to measure the amount of time remaining on a bond: maturity date and yield to maturity. When looking at funds, you'll often see the average maturity date of its bonds. But there's a far more important measure for bond funds; it's called *duration*.

I'll be quite honest at this point and say that duration is a difficult concept to explain. Pretty frequently, people writing about bonds just punt when it comes to explaining bond duration. They use the term synonymously with average maturity. This is a mistake. Whereas maturity is a measurement of the time remaining till a bond is redeemed, duration is a direct measure of interest rate risk. If interest rates move up by 1 percent and a bond has a duration of five years, the value of the bond will drop by 5 percent. If interest rates drop by 1 percent, the same bond will gain 5 percent in value. Average maturity doesn't offer a similarly specific predictive value.

How is the duration calculation made? Duration looks at the coupon rate and principal payment to determine the length of time needed to recover the full cost of the bond. The math gets pretty complicated, and there's no need for you to memorize the formulas. However, if you want a more detailed explanation of duration, as well as a look at the underlying math of a duration calculation, I recommend this page at Investopedia: http://www.investopedia.com/university/advancedbond/advancedbond5.asp.

The point to take out of this discussion is that when you look at different funds, you absolutely must look beyond average maturity when comparing them; duration is the far better measure.

The Bond Fund Manager's Lament

Bond funds clearly aren't as sexy as stock funds. Some superstar fund manager might make some great trades that put its fund well ahead of others in its sector. There's a natural mystery in what's going to happen to a given corporation over time. It may fly or sink on a new product release. But that doesn't translate to the bond world. Bonds are bonds and every bond fund manager is looking at the same sets of bonds with known rates of return. So it's pretty tough for one fund to seriously outperform another that takes on similar bonds of similar duration. If you keep this in mind—that there often isn't much difference between bonds of a similar type—then you're bound to make some good decisions.

Looking Past Yield

Scanning the Internet, you can find all kinds of stories of bond funds that have tried to lure in investors by claiming an unusually high yield. Typically, a fund looking to create a better impression in its marketing literature will throw some lower quality higher-yield bonds in with its core holdings. It's sleazy business, but something you need to be aware of. If a bond fund is offering substantially higher yield than others with similar attributes, something's fishy.

The Key Issue in Bond Funds

Bond funds are so similar that the greatest distinguishing factor between them is usually the management fee. A fund that charges an exorbitant fee can't even hope to make up the difference by investing more cleverly than his peers. It just isn't possible. So you really want to zero in on the management fee once you've decided on a class of bond that you want within your fund.

A Bond Fund Listing

Let's take a quick look at a listing for a fund that's pretty well respected, the Vanguard Intermediate-Term Treasury Admiral, which trades under the ticker symbol VFIUX. I've grabbed this information from Yahoo! Finance, which is free to use.

FUND OVERVIEW	
Category:	Intermediate Government
Fund Family:	Vanguard
Net Assets:	2.43B
Year-to-Date Return:	2.72%
Yield:	4.80%
Morningstar Rating:	★★★★★
Fund Inception Date:	12-Feb-01

MORNINGSTAR STYLE BOX

Intermediate Government
[View Category Definition]

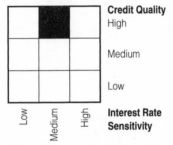

Credit Quality
High

Medium

Low

Low Medium High

Interest Rate Sensitivity

View Top Intermediate Government Funds
About the Morningstar Style Box

MANAGEMENT INFORMATION

David R. Glocke
Lead Manager since 29-May-01

Glocke is principal and portfolio manager with Vanguard Group, his employer since 1997. He has worked in investment management since 1991.

FUND SUMMARY

The investment seeks to provide a moderate and sustainable level of current income. The fund normally invests at least 80% of assets in U.S. Treasury bills, notes and bonds issued by U.S. Treasury. It is expected to maintain a dollar-weighted average maturity of 5 to 10 years.

FUND OPERATIONS	
Last Dividend (31-Aug-07):	0.04
Last Cap Gain (29-Dec-05):	0.06
Annual Holdings Turnover	87.00%
Average for Category:	226.99%

FEES & EXPENSES

Expense	VFIUX	Category Avg
Total Expense Ratio:	0.10%	1.09%
Max 12b1 Fee:	0.00%	N/A
Max Front End Sales Load:	0.00%	4.25%
Max Deferred Sales Load:	0.00%	2.68%
3 Yr Expense Projection*:	$32	$513
5 Yr Expense Projection*:	$56	$761
10 Yr Expense Projection*:	$128	$1,472

Figure 11.1

This isn't everything you need to know, but it's a good start, and there are some very encouraging signs. The Morningstar five-star rating lets you know that it's been performing in the top 10 percent of its sector. This isn't the most telling statistic, but it's not a bad sign. What I really like about what I see here is the expense ratio of 0.1 percent. That's very low, and probably a good part of the reason it's been able to return more than others. Notice that the average within the category is almost a full percentage point higher.

TOP 10 HOLDINGS (68.42% OF TOTAL ASSETS)			
Company	Symbol	% Assets	YTD Return %
U.S. Treasury Bond 8.75%	N/A	13.77	N/A
U.S. Treasury Note 4.5%	N/A	10.06	N/A
U.S. Treasury Note 3.625%	N/A	9.75	N/A
U.S. Treasury Note 4.25%	N/A	8.68	N/A
U.S. Treasury Note 4%	N/A	6.09	N/A
U.S. Treasury Note 4%	N/A	4.99	N/A
U.S. Treasury Note	N/A	4.38	N/A
U.S. Treasury Note 3.875%	N/A	3.71	N/A
Private Expt Fdg 7.25%	N/A	3.63	N/A
U.S. Treasury Bond 8.875%	N/A	3.36	N/A

Figure 11.2

BOND RATINGS (%)		
Sector	VFIUX	Category Avg
U.S. Government	N/A	N/A
AAA	100.00	97.94
AA	0.00	0.72
A	0.00	0.17
BBB	0.00	0.20
BB	0.00	0.00
B	0.00	0.00
Below B	0.00	0.02
Other	0.00	0.94

BOND HOLDINGS		
Averages	VFIUX	Category Avg
Maturity	6.50	7.04
Duration	5.16	4.29
Credit Quality	AAA	AAA

Figure 11.3

Here you see that the holdings are about as safe as you could ask for: You've got 100 percent AAA bonds, with an average duration of 5.16 years. You can also look at some research reports, which confirm the conclusion that this fund is pretty tough to beat.

In contrast, you can find funds—I'm not going to name names here—where there are pretty similar holdings but annual charges of over 1 percent. If that weren't enough, some charge front-end loads of about 5 percent. If anyone *ever* suggests that you pay a load on a bond fund, tell him to take a flying leap.

Individual Bonds Versus Bond Funds

What's better for you—bond funds or individual bonds? It really depends on a couple of factors. Do you need steady income over a defined period of time? Then purchase bonds outright. When you buy bonds outright, you'll know exactly what coupon payments you'll be receiving, so you can plan accurately around them. Bonds are also an excellent choice when you need to amass a specific amount of money over a period of time. For example, if you're looking to start a fund for your child's college tuition, you might not want to expose the investment to the ups and downs of stocks or even the volatility of interest rates that can cause bond funds to deliver a poor return.

Bond funds, however, are preferable in a couple of circumstances. If you want to reinvest your coupons so that you gain more shares of your fund, bond funds will be much easier to work with. (Depending on the size of your investment, your coupons on individual bonds may not be enough to reinvest.) Bond funds also allow for diversification that would be tough to do with individual bonds. Say you want to buy into corporate bonds with a little more risk and a bit more potential return. That's fine, but you don't want to plop down any meaningful percentage of your income on any one even slightly risky bond offering. You want to spread that risk out over many corporate bonds, and bond funds are by far the easiest way to go about that.

WAXIE'S SIDEBAR: The Bond Ladder

A popular technique and useful technique for those nearing retirement is called the bond ladder. You'd do this by buying Treasuries with varying maturity dates, from one year to ten years. Your goal is to have bonds expiring every year while having an average maturity rate of about five years. In one year, when those first bonds are redeemed, you reinvest in ten-year Treasuries; the following year you do the same with the bonds that come due then. By reinvesting every year, you maintain an average five-year maturity date.

There are a couple of solid advantages to using a bond ladder. First is that you don't get locked into an interest rate for an extended period of time. Should the bond rates increase, you won't have all your money tied into a single long-term bond. Should bond rates fall, you'll already be locked into a decent rate on many of your bonds. Note that you can't create a bond ladder solely with Treasuries purchased directly from the government. The government issues bonds that mature in 1, 2, 5, and 10 years. So to get bonds that will mature in 6, 7, 8, and 9 years, you'll need to go your broker and the secondary market.

Elsewhere in Fixed Income

This chapter has concentrated on bonds. But bonds are part of a larger category called fixed income. The other major entrant in the fixed income category is the certificate of deposit (CD). A CD is really a lot like a bond in that it's a debt obligation that pays a specific rate of interest. The debt in the case of a CD is being floated by your bank. They'll use the debt to fund mortgages and other ventures.

Banks generally sell CDs as offering some advantages over money market and savings accounts when you don't need immediate access to your money. You lock in a higher rate of return than a money market for a year or two or five, and the money is FDIC insured.

But CDs are by and large a lazy investment. You throw your money in them because they're easy; you can do it at your bank, no muss, no fuss. However, just about any time you're considering a CD, you should be looking to bonds or bond funds. With bonds you get to choose your tax obligation, whereas all CDs are taxable. Most CDs have penalties if you get at your money before the maturity date. This isn't the case with a bond fund. Most important, you can make more from a bond or bond fund purchase than a CD. If you're going to tie your money up for a fixed rate of return over a year or two or five, get as much out of it as you can. Buy a Treasury or something else that fits your needs.

Quiz

1. **The amount the bondholder receives upon maturity is known as:**

   a. Par value

   b. Purchase price

   c. Original value

   d. Final value

   Answer: a

2. **As the interest rate goes up, what happens to the price of bonds on the open market?**

   a. It goes up

   b. It goes down

   Answer: b

3. *Which term measures the interest paid on a bond when compared to par value?*

a. Yield

b. Yield to maturity

c. Coupon rate

Answer: c

4. *The issuer of a callable bond reserves what right?*

a. To make adjustments to interest rate depending on the action of the Federal Reserve

b. To pay the bondholder par value and stop issuing interest payments

c. To increase the duration of the bond

Answer: b

5. *The U.S. government bonds with the shortest times to maturity are known as:*

a. T-bills

b. Treasury notes

c. Treasury bonds

Answer: a

6. *Which of the following entities issues triple tax-free bonds?*

a. U.S. Treasury

b. States

c. Corporations

Answer: b

7. *According to Morningstar, short-term bond funds concentrate on bonds with how much time to maturity?*

a. 1–2 years

b. 1–5 years

c. 1–7 years

d. 1–10 years

Answer: b

8. *True or false, CDs have tax advantages over certain bonds.*

a. True

b. False

Answer: b

Chapter 12

The Almighty Buck

Cash is, indeed, *king!*

Throughout this book I spend a lot of time talking about ways to be active with your retirement account(s). Sometimes being active means being "inactive." I'll explain. Read on. As the saying goes, "You gotta know when to hold 'em, know when to fold 'em." Well, cash plays a very important role in any portfolio, and in any retirement account. There are going to be many times when you simply have no solid idea which way the market, bonds, or other personal things in your life are going. It's okay. We all go through that. I sure do. Life is about making adjustments and learning from your mistakes, or even better, from others' mistakes so you never have to make them yourself!

I have a saying I tell my clients at trendfund.com all the time—when in doubt, stay out! Or when in doubt do nothing, just sit on your hands. There's no shame in not being clear, there is shame in not being clear and then losing your hard-earned money and/or putting your retirement funds at risk! If you want to gamble, go to Vegas, don't ruin your retirement.

Cash plays an integral role, particularly the way the market volatility has been the last few years. And as I write this book there have been several bank failures, and by the time you read this there will probably be quite a few more. So, given the uncertainty that will probably be with us for a long while (though ya never know!), when I say "cash" it carries a different meaning today than it did five years ago, or than it may mean five years from now. I like the idea of having your retirement money at potentially the only truly safe haven we have here in the United States, and that's directly with the U.S. Treasury. You can easily open a direct account there at http://www.treasurydirect.gov. It's very simple and in my view a lot safer than any bank out there. Of course there is always the chance that the entire country will go bankrupt, but if that happens we'll have a lot bigger issues to worry about! So, let's be optimistic that at the very least the Treasury won't fold!

WAXIE'S TIP

Put your cash in as safe a haven as possible. Remember, you only have one retirement and you need to rule it! Go to http://www.treasurydirect.gov and open a direct account with the Treasury to avoid the potential that whomever you bank with has issues that hurt you!

Other Uses of Cash

Cash is a good equalizer, meaning that it can help you balance out your retirement portfolio. I like to have *some* cash on hand at all times. That way I can always do something to protect anything else I might be doing. Some people use gold and other commodities in that capacity, but I think cash is always the simplest and best way ultimately. One thing I don't recommend is trading commodities with money earmarked for your retirement. That's something that would be way too aggressive even for me.

Also, if you think about it, most of the money in the stock market made on the long side (investing) is made in brief spurts during the year. Many people swear by certain timing systems that say things like, "sell in May and go away." And there's a reason these trends, which I track at trendfund.com, work much of the time. They don't work all the time. But they don't have to. The idea is to give your retirement an edge, right? So, if something works much of the time, then it needs to be respected, at least. You might find it appropriate at times to have *all* your retirement monies in *cash* (Treasuries). There's nothing wrong with making 3 to 5 percent guaranteed on your money. Absolutely nothing. And it's certainly better than forcing the issue and losing money. It's amazing how many times I tell clients and friends or family that they should put their money in a money market account or Treasuries instead of just tossing their money into the stock market. Inevitably their response? "I don't want to make three percent on my money! I *need* to make more than that!" Well, since the stock market has gone *down* over the last decade overall (I'm assuming that will still be the case when you read this) you may *need* to make more than 3 percent on your money, but chances are you would be down dramatically. It's better to make 3 percent than lose *any* percent!

....
WAXIE'S TIP

There's nothing wrong with *cash*, it's often *king!* Better to make a small percent than lose! Cash is a good tool to help you Rule Your Freakin' Retirement!

Gold and Commodities

I get asked my opinion on gold a lot. I called gold a lot higher when it was $275 an ounce. I've owned my share of gold coins. I still have a few. I'm not a huge believer in gold as an alternative to much of anything. It could go up, it could go down. It's no longer tied, at least right now, to the U.S. dollar. If you want to own some gold, that's your call. Just remember that if the economy stays slow, which I believe it probably will, and if we go into a deflationary time, which I believe we probably will, then gold will probably go way down with all the rest of the commodities. If, though, we start moving into an inflationary period, which is possible, then gold could be a nice hedge and something you want to own, even if just to have it. It's nice and shiny, and everyone, including me, thinks it's pretty cool to have some gold bullion or coins lying around!

If you want to get involved in commodities trading, this isn't the place for a meaningful discussion, but what I will say is that people do need to *eat!* That is why I worry about gold being viable long term. It may retain much of its monetary value, but also remember that in a slowing economy luxury items, like fancy jewelry, become a lot less important. If gold sales were to dwindle, then surely the price would drop.

If you want to own gold, I would just buy a small amount and keep it for a rainy day. I would trade it, but I would not own that much of it outright for the future. While it may go higher, I'm not a believer in it at the time of writing. Hey, it could be $2,500 an ounce when you get to reading this, so you can say I was wrong. Be my guest! Or it could go back to $250 an ounce. When things are a toss-up I try to not play them long or short, but rather stay neutral.

But, like I said—It is nice and shiny!

Chapter 13

Asset Allocation

Are you ready to finally start putting that money and that knowledge to work, dudes and dudesses? Good! At this point in the book, we've talked mostly about receptacles and vehicles. Receptacles are the accounts—the IRAs and 401(k)s and 529s—the places that hold your money. The vehicles are the investment products themselves—the stocks and mutual funds and bonds and bond funds and annuities. You needed to be grounded in those areas first. But the real exciting times come when, armed with your new knowledge, you decide exactly how to deal with the assets you have at your disposal. You're going to war, you are now armed—locked and loaded. Let's rumble!

Rumbling comes down to a simple question: What exactly should I buy, and how much of it should I buy? But like many simple questions, this one has a complicated answer. In fact, it will take the remainder of this chapter to get you moving toward an answer that works best for you.

What the Rest of the Financial Planning World Says

It should be pretty clear by now that I don't believe in much of the "common wisdom" about investing. If that's not clear, then I need to do a quick rewrite and make sure you got it when I said that I think most investment advisors suck. Pop open just about any book on retirement planning, or go to any investor-related Web site and you'll see one worldview repeated again and again. These investment "experts" look at the history of the stock market, the benchmarks and indexes by which it's measured, and they draw a conclusion: The stock market will inevitably go up over time. Sure, there will be nasty downswings along the way. But if you have a long enough time horizon, you can wait out the downturns and see a nice profit. The better financial planners say the time horizon should be measured in years, or even better decades, as there is plenty of risk along the way.

Believing rising stock prices are inevitable, financial planners recommend that you put your money into stocks for your long-term investing. But caution is recommended, because any single stock could be a dog. So, if you are going to get into the market, stock mutual funds are the investment of choice. They at least give you a broad exposure to a lot of stocks. Beyond the exposure offered by any single fund, planners insist that you spread out your investment over many different types of companies and many different areas of the world. You ought to include funds that concentrate on mid-size, small, and foreign companies.

While stocks hold a primary place in your investments for most of your life, they're not the be-all and end-all of investing. Bonds and cash are also important. Bonds, with their known returns and minimal risk, provide a strong element of stability while still delivering some profit.

These are the basic tools: stock and stock funds, bonds and bond funds, and cash. How much you put in each depends on your tolerance for risk. If you're young and daring, why not put nearly all of your money in stocks and stock funds (actively managing it yourself). And while you're at it, why not take some fliers on stock funds that are risky, but could really kick some ass in the long term. As you get older, though, you want to be less exposed to downturns in the market. So as you near retirement it's best to move your money to bonds and cash.

Along the way, you'll have specific percentages that you'll try to stick to. Keeping to specific percentages has an advantage beyond keeping you within your risk tolerance. It's easiest to explain this advantage by giving an example. Say you have $200,000 invested at a fifty-fifty allocation—half in bonds, half in stocks. Then stocks take a tumble—they drop by 30 percent. Your portfolio loses value obviously. You still have roughly $100,000 in bonds, but now you only have $70,000 in stocks. To get back to your desired fifty-fifty allocation, you'd have to move some money from bonds to stocks. Moving $15,000 would give you $85,000 in each category.

By making this move, you'll be putting money into the stock market when it's down. Stocks will be cheaper and presumably a better value. Conversely, when stocks go up you'll be cashing out, taking profit at a time when there are fewer bargains to be found in the market. As always, this is contingent on your being active. Just because a stock or fund is down doesn't automatically make it a good time to get in. There are many times when the bad gets worse. A general rule to follow is that the *hot* sectors tend to stay hot until, well, until they don't! In 2007 the Dry Bulk stocks (DRYS, EGLE) were red hot all year. In 2008 (and some of 2007) fertilizer stocks were hot, at least mid-way through the year. Stocks like Monsanto (MON), Mosaic (MOS), and Agruim (AGU) were buyable on any dips. *Both* tanked hard mid-2008! New, hot stocks will emerge in the next bull run.

. . . .
WAXIE'S TIP

Buy low and sell high only works if you are a seer. I prefer to buy high and sell higher! Hot stocks and sectors tend to stay hot for a while. Stick with the winners; they usually win more! I use the baseball analogy often: If your team is down by one run and down to its last out, do you want Ryan Howard or Omar Visquel? You want your power dude up there! He's your best shot to knock one out of the yard!

However, many financial planners do not want you to trade actively—far from it. This sort of balancing of the portfolio, they say, is something that should be done *twice a year*. According to them, you shouldn't be trading frequently; you shouldn't be making constant adjustments. To them, trading actively is gambling, not investing. With the exception of your annual or biannual rebalancing, you're not supposed to touch your investments. Wait out the down times, they say. Don't try to second-guess the markets.

WAXIE'S SIDEBAR: Dollar Cost Averaging

How should you move your money into investment products? One commonly mentioned strategy is called dollar cost averaging (DCA). The concept is very simple. Using DCA, you invest a specific amount in a product, say a stock fund, every month. So if you have $10,000 to invest, you don't throw it in the fund you're interested in all at once. Rather, you do it $1,000 at a time over ten months. The potential advantage is that, over that time, you don't risk dumping all of your money into a stock or a fund while it's overvalued. You may buy ten shares at a high price one month and fifteen at a lower price a couple of months later. In the end, you pay the average cost of the stock over that period of time.

Often, DCA is talked about as a way of maintaining discipline in savings. It's sort of like the "pay yourself first" philosophy I talked about in chapter 2.

Is DCA a good idea for you? If it helps you maintain your discipline in saving, by all means. But I'm not at all convinced that DCA makes any sense for a long-term investor with cash to invest. You don't have to do a lot of research before you come across a number of articles and papers that share the idea that DCA makes little sense in most markets. This research looks at historical data to test the effectiveness of DCA. But beyond that, I think there's a very basic logic problem with DCA. If you think a fund is a good buy for the long haul—say twenty years or more, and you're expecting a decent return, how big a downside could you possibly be seeing by investing now, rather than over ten months? Why miss out on the potential gains over the DCA period? A short downslide is all but meaningless, and time is on your side. I mean, isn't that the logic of long-term investing?

So, if you want the fund for the long haul and have the cash, just put your money in and be done with it. You can check out this article at MSN for additional explanations: http://moneycentral.msn.com/content/ P104966.asp. Many believe that DCA is simply a marketing gimmick used by investment houses to convince skittish investors that by wading in slowly they don't risk drowning. DCA could also generate additional fees for brokers, sometimes significant ones.

Some Typical Allocations

Ready for some exciting pie graphs? Good. They're coming.

Most financial planners recommend a pretty high percentage of stocks. You'll often see an equation that suggests that an investor should subtract his or her age from 110 to determine the proper allocation. That's the percentage the investor should have in stocks. The remainder should be in fixed income and cash, in roughly equal amounts.

The following graph shows a basic allocation for someone who is forty years old.

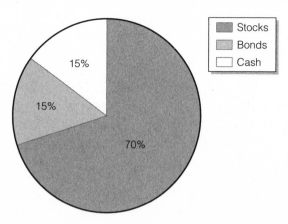

Figure 13.1

A more detailed allocation would provide a breakdown of how the stock portion of the pie is invested. A typical calculation would look something like Figure 13.2, with 25 percent in large-cap holdings, and roughly 15 percent each in mid-cap, small-cap, international, bonds, and cash.

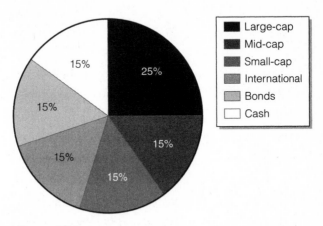

Figure 13.2

As you age, your risk tolerance decreases. To keep things less volatile you'd move gradually out of stocks and rely more on bonds and cash. In your stock holdings you'd have a higher percentage of large-cap domestic stocks. The following figure shows

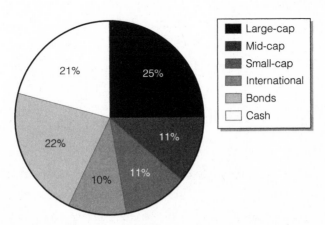

Figure 13.3

an allocation for someone who is fifty-five years old and has significant savings.

This allocation has roughly 55 percent in stocks, half of that in large-cap funds. The remainder is divided between bonds and cash, with roughly half in each.

....

WAXIE'S NOTE

I came up with these sample allocations by looking at several sources. Charles Schwab, T. Rowe Price, Fidelity, and other investment houses have worksheets that get pretty specific in determining risk. If you're interested in going with this kind of allocation, I encourage you to go to one of these investment houses and do the worksheets. In pulling together these numbers, I also looked at the IPERS retirement calculator (http://www.ipers.org/calcs/AssetAllocator.html) and Henry Hebeler's book, *Getting Started in a Financially Secure Retirement* (Wiley, 2007).

....

Auto Allocation

The larger investment houses know that there are a number of people out there who have no real interest in maintaining their accounts. They don't want to bother moving from stocks to funds over time or choosing funds within different sectors. These folks would do pretty well to look at target-date funds. A target-date fund is simply a fund that spreads its investments in other funds. Over time, as the fund ages, the allocation changes from riskier stocks to less-risky stocks, bonds, and cash.

For example, the T. Rowe Price Retirement 2035 Fund is geared to people looking to retire around that year. The money in the 2035 fund is pushed out to several other T. Rowe Price funds. In 2007, the 2035 fund held 88 percent stocks, 7 percent bonds, and a small amount of cash. A full 20 percent of the entire investment was in international stock. This is a reasonably aggressive, somewhat risky portfolio, I think. In time, the allocation will move to look more like the T. Rowe Retirement 2010 Fund, which has 62 percent in stocks and 36 percent in cash and bonds. The expense ratio is a pretty reasonable 0.76 percent on the 2035 fund; the cost of the 2010 is a little lower. There are no additional fees for the underlying fees.

Fidelity, Vanguard, and others have funds with targeted retirement dates. Vanguard target-date funds, unsurprisingly, invest in a number of index funds, which help keep costs very low. As of 2007, the Vanguard Target Retirement 2035 Fund had 90 percent of its investments in stock index funds and 10 percent in bond index funds. In 2035, the fund will have 50 percent bonds and 50 percent stocks. And in 2045, the fund will be even more heavily weighted in bonds.

Risks in the Typical Allocations

Imagine we're back in 2001 and you have $1 million in a fund similar to the Vanguard Target Retirement funds, and you're planning on retiring in 2003. In February of 2001, you're probably feeling really good about your prospects. The index funds have done well enough for you, and with $1 million you feel you can live a lifestyle you're happy with. Just work a few more years, and you'll be ready to go. You may even feel that the fifty-fifty allocation between bonds and stocks that you've chosen is too conservative, but you don't want to be greedy, so you stick with it.

Then the markets tank. In one horrible day in October 2002 you look at your account and see that your $1 million is now worth just over $800,000. (Thank God for that 50 percent in bonds.) Friends who had more aggressive portfolios, more heavily weighted in tech, have been absolutely flattened. They've put off retirement indefinitely, and you have no idea what to do. You've lost a ton of money—a full 20 percent—and that's enough to make you reconsider what you can and can't do. Is retirement still possible but at a different income level? What if the markets don't recover? What can you do?

This is the problem I have with most of the typical allocation algorithms. I don't think they take seriously enough the consequences of an ill-timed steep downturn. What if the market dives 35 percent or more, as it did in 2002, when you're sixty-three and two years away from retiring? Even if you use the commonly suggested allocations, you'll have over 40 percent of your money in stocks. You'll lose a significant portion of your portfolio. At that point, you'll have to figure out whether you can wait out a market recovery that may never happen. Or you might have to consider whether retirement at that point will eat into your principal, thereby endangering your lifestyle for years to come.

Allocating the Waxie Way

At this point I want to talk about some alternative methods of spreading your money around. I want you to think about how you, by using your own wits and intelligence, can make the most of your retirement income. I want you to be creative, as well as realistic and disciplined and risk-aware.

Become Your Own Hedge Fund

For starters, why not spend some time looking to become a financial baron. You hear about hedge funds all the time, and some of them rack up *huge* gains year after year. You could try to become Steven Cohen of SAC Capital Partners. He's a world-renowned billionaire who made his money running a hedge fund. You can do some of what he does in your IRA.

To start thinking like a hedge fund manager you just need to be aware of the investment opportunities you encounter. Say you like a small-cap stock that you've read about, or maybe you're a fan of their products. You can buy the stock outright, rather than a fund or an ETF, and you can trade it or hold it for the long haul. Pick companies you like that have products that you admire and have a large percentage of their given market. Read about the company and its competitors; there's a wealth of information on the Internet. Before too long you may find yourself something of an expert on a small market sector. Trust me, it's not going to be long before you know a *whole* lot more than most brokers you'd deal with.

This is more or less the Peter Lynch approach (and sort of what Warren Buffett does as well). Say your wife likes Coach bags and you see lines out the door whenever you shop there. You may want to pick up some shares, or even buy some call options on the stock.

Become a Trend Trader

I've said it often enough in these pages for you to get the point: I've made a lot of money trading, and everything I have comes from my ability to recognize likely short-term movements in the market. I've done it well, and I've taught bunches of other people to do it well. I have two other books on the topic (*Rule the Freakin' Markets* and *Power Trading/Power Living*). Through trendfund.com I've taught thousands of people to make great money in the market.

I'll talk a lot more about my philosophies and techniques in the next chapters. But for this chapter, which is about allocation, it's important to understand that there are options beyond mutual funds, bonds, and cash.

WAXIE'S ALLOCATIONS

Forget what the typical allocations are: What are some of *my* ideas on this subject? Well, for one thing, I don't like the idea of passive investments. As I am typing this, *all* the stock markets around the world are roiled in pain. Investors everywhere are being told it's "Too late to sell!"

and "The market will come back, it always does!" and my favorite "This is the buying opportunity of a lifetime!" Well, maybe by the time you pick this book up and get to this point the stock market will be a safe haven for investors worldwide! Maybe the credit crisis will be proven as a myth, and maybe we'll be at new all-time highs on the Dow, headed to 25,000 as some pundits would have you believe. Anything is possible in life, that I am sure of. Same as: One day hell may actually really freeze over!

Regardless, though, I think the notion that the stock market is something that should carry so much weight in your retirement plans is foolish, at best. Why? Because even if the markets do rally to new highs at some point, now or in fifty years, it is likely to be with new and different leadership. So, even if that happened it's very likely that the stocks you own as blue chips won't give you the same bang for your buck as these new leaders. Just look at the stock prices of Cisco, Dell, IBM, Yahoo!, and others as examples. In the great bull run the market had in the late '90s those stocks led the way higher. If you look at their stock prices in the next bull run that went from 2003 to 2007, you'll find that those stocks weren't anywhere near their peaks, while the Dow and S&P were at all-time highs. That's mainly due to the fact that the S&P 500 is constantly changing its makeup. What are considered blue chips today, may be potato chips a year or two from now! And, as I've stated many times to my clients and my blog readers, even without that, it is false to say that the market historically *always* goes up over a long period of time. That's a very skewed way of looking at things. It's also self-serving since the majority of fund managers are "long only" funds, meaning they can only buy stocks, they can't short or hedge their investments.

So, having said all that, my idea would be, as you may have ascertained, to be much more active with your money and handle your own retirement. You know your needs better than anyone, including me. If you are young I'd have something like the following:

- 15 percent stocks (both long and potentially short using ETFs that are ultra-short the market)

- 25 percent interest bearing cash
- 25 percent bonds

35% actively manage trading capital. This would include some of the strategies discussed in this book, and perhaps some riskier trades on commodities. I haven't spent much time on these in this book, but I think they are starting to get a much broader acceptance and I suspect that it won't be that long before more of the general public becomes savvy about how to trade them. If you do ever trade them, please make sure you know enough about them to risk your retirement on the price of corn or soybeans, or pork bellies!

Many of my clients tell me they trade the components of their IRA often, or even as their primary trading account. Some of them have done quite well. We get a ton of testimonials at trendfund.com, and I'm always happy when I get one about an IRA. It means one less person worried about retirement and one more client Ruling their Freakin' Retirement!

But what if you are a bit older and let's say within ten or so years of retiring? Well, I would say that you want something like the following:

- 35 percent interest bearing cash or Treasuries
- 45 percent bonds
- 20 percent actively managing your account with covered calls and perhaps some market timing strategies using trends that you have studied and proven out consistently.

Notice that I would not have any money in the stock market. Yes, I know, I know, I'm a nut! I've seen one too many close-to-retirees get clobbered and have to put off retirement because they were over-invested in so-called "safe" stocks. I'm sorry, I just don't see any stock being safe at all. What does that mean? We've learned over the last couple of years that companies that have been around for literally decades, if not a century, can go out of business just the same as a poorly placed pizza parlor! Need I point out Lehman Brothers, Bear Stearns, Washington Mutual, and probably quite a few more after I wrote this!

As I write, the stock market hasn't gone *anywhere* in over ten years! It's *down* dramatically from where it was ten years ago when it hit 12,000 on the Dow. Maybe it'll be 15,000 by the time you read this, but even if that were the case, which I doubt, the timing of your retirement is too reliant on it being a good market, and that's just a wee bit too much risk for me! As I near retirement I suspect I will be even more active with my account. Not more aggressive or risky; in fact. I'm someone who thinks the more active you are in managing something, the more control you have over the positive results sure to follow! As I've stated a few times—*no* market goes up forever and not every stock, or market comes back and stays back forever either! Don't get lulled in by every market rally, or every market drop as though it has much meaning. It doesn't, and putting blind faith in anyone but yourself, in my opinion, is a recipe for failure! This is about Ruling Your Freakin' Retirement, not letting someone else ruin it!

WAXIE'S TIP

The more active you are at managing your retirement, the more successful it should be! While not everyone has the time or inclination to aggressively trade or take risks with their hard-earned money, if you do it correctly, I would argue that you are actually *safer* managing your own money.

Asset allocation is key to ruling your retirement, and the only way I know to really figure that out is doing your own due diligence, and like most other things in life, trial and error. I can't honestly sit here and tell you, "Hey, dude or dudes, you should have 10 percent this, and 20 percent that!" you need to take a deep breath, and prepare for your own risk tolerance and goals. You know them a lot better than I can know them. I'm not advocating you to rush out and trade your IRA; what I am suggesting is that you need to be aware of where you are at. I know people who have no clue whether the funds they own in their IRA are up, down, or doing nothing at all! That, to me, is just not acceptable. Not at all.

Quiz

1. **The process by which you spread a buy of a stock or fund out over many months is known as:**

   a. Dollar cost averaging

   b. Incremental buying

   c. Broker benefit program

   d. One share, one month

   Answer: a

2. **According to typical allocation principles, approximately what percentage of a retirement fund should be in stocks and stock funds when the person is thirty years from retirement?**

   a. 50 percent

   b. 60 percent

   c. 75 percent

   d. 85 percent

   Answer: d

3. **Using the same principles, approximately what percentage of your funds should you have in stocks when you are just a few years away from retirement?**

   a. 30 percent

   b. 40 percent

   c. 50 percent

   d. 60 percent

   Answer: c

4. **Waxie's alternatives to the typical allocation include which of the following?**

   a. Looking for investment opportunities in your own areas of interest

   b. Trading the fluctuations in the market

   c. Creating your own index fund

   d. Putting large bets on black 24

   Answers: a, b

Part III

Making the Most of It

Chapter 14

Looking to Trends

....
WAXIE'S TIP: Trends Are Your Friends!

What we've talked about so far—bonds, bond funds, and stocks funds—are great tools. Most of the readers of this book are using them now and will use them in the future. After reading the chapters I've offered on those subjects, you'll be better equipped to make the most out of your bond and fund purchases. But here's the thing: I've made millions in the markets, and I didn't make a dime of it by putting my cash into funds and waiting for a good return. In fact, I am not, nor have I ever been, an "investor." That's what people who buy stocks and funds for the sake of holding them are—investors.

I'm a trader, and with my company, trendfund.com, I've taught thousands of others to be traders as well. Many of these people have made a *lot* of money. I call what I do "trend trading." I look to the market for repeating patterns—things that happen with great regularity. Believe me when I tell you that there are repeating patterns in the markets that can be spotted and exploited for profit. Of course, nothing in the market is foolproof or guaranteed—not even close. But if you're observant and diligent, you can spot patterns that lead to likely outcomes. If you buy and sell carefully, you can profit off a trend when it comes to fruition and minimize your loss when it doesn't. In the end your gains should outpace your losses and you'll make a good bit of income on your trend trading.

Why do these predictable patterns, these trends, exist? They're available in the market because the market is run by people. And people tend to make similar decisions repeatedly when confronted with similar situations. Think about your dating history for a minute: Do you see any repeated patterns? Maybe you really go for redheads or sharp dressers or blondes over brunettes. Whatever, it doesn't really matter. What does matter is that most everyone has patterns, or habits, that they repeat often. Chances are that through your life you've been attracted to a physical or psychological type, and you're drawn to this sort of person over and over. There may be some exceptions in your dating history. You may normally go for the rugged outdoorsy type, but spend some pleasant months with an uptight desk-bound lawyer. These things happen. But it doesn't change the fact that your tendency is to go for those who like hiking, skiing, and Subaru wagons. I'd go into my dating tendencies, but that would take up a whole book in and of itself and I don't think most of you would want to pay to read that! If you want, you can go to the local Blockbuster video store and pick up my first movie, though, *Crazy for Love.* It's a romantic comedy, a dark one!

Regardless, it works similarly with the market. People do the same things over and over. Not always, but often enough that you can make reasonable (and profitable) predictions of future behavior.

There are hundreds of different trends, and to take full advantage of all the ones that I know of, you'd have to devote a lot of time and resources to trend trading. Many trendfund.com clients, not to mention the company's staff, trade from the market's opening to the market's close every day. However, I realize that most of the readers of this book aren't looking to ditch their careers in order to become full-time traders. You don't want to wake up to CNBC and spend the day watching the movement of various stocks and indexes. You picked up this book so you could get some tips on how to make your retirement plans more secure.

Even on this limited basis, trends can be really helpful. There are several trends that I'll talk about in this section that don't require full-time attention. Using these techniques will require substantially more time than an invest-and-hold strategy, but it's not going to eat up the entirety of your week. Some of these trends you could play every few weeks, others you could play daily, or as often as you want to.

The time spent on learning and executing these trend trades will be well worth the effort. You'll have a level of control over your money that can't be approached by any fund. And the potential returns from trend trades are really terrific. This stuff may sound scary at first, but it's well worth a shot.

Seasonal Trends

Some of the trends I discuss in this book can be played pretty much every day. Gaps (chapter 15) occur every single day the market is open. Opportunities to play options (chapter 16) are also available on an ongoing basis. But some of the other trends that I like the most are only available at specific times of the year. In this chapter, I'll discuss three seasonal trends.

Earnings Runners

I want to start this discussion of trends by looking at one of my favorite trends, the Earnings Runner trend. It's among the most reliable trends that I know of, and it's one that won't require you to spend all day every day in front of a computer, watching the movement of stocks.

As I mentioned, a trend is something that happens repeatedly and regularly. A trend develops because people do the same things for the same reasons. Two of the greatest motivators of human behavior are hope and fear. Chicago Cubs fans, for example, go out to Wrigley Field every year, even when history tells them nothing good is going to happen. But they continue to go because at some level they're hopeful. They *believe* things can go well. Hope is a powerful human motivator. And, hey, with the team the Cubbies have now, they may actually win a World Series. . . . We'll see, they'll have to get past my Mets first!

Nowhere in the market is hope more evident than in the Earnings Runner trend. Every fiscal quarter, publicly traded companies must tell the world how they're doing. They release statements that tell analysts and the public how much they've made or lost in the previous three months, along with a fair amount of detail as to how they made or lost money. For some companies and their stocks, earnings announcements aren't much cause for excitement. A big, stable company that hasn't changed its business much in a dozen years and hasn't seen any real change will more than likely release an earnings statement much like the one before it. Ho-hum.

This is not the case for many stocks. Some stocks and industry sectors, particularly those that are seen to have a lot of upside potential, produce a lot of excitement around earnings time. There's hope that these companies will have something dazzling to report. Often they don't, but still the hope is there. The hope is reflected in the stock price as the trading public awaits the announcement of earnings. Last chapter I spoke about so-called hot stocks. These stocks are usually the best stocks for this trend because they generate the most buzz at earnings time.

Fiscal quarters conclude toward the end of March, June, September, and December. A short time after the close of a quarter, companies release their earnings reports. Third-quarter earnings reports, for example, come out around the middle of October. The stocks that generate a lot of optimism and hope will often see a nice rise in the stock price prior to that earnings report.

Take a look at what happened to a well-known and highly traded stock like eBay prior to a recent earnings report. The following chart shows the price of eBay's stock a couple of weeks before and a few days after its October 2007 earnings report. You can see a nice spike in price just before the October 18 announcement. The stock then lost a good deal of value after announcing poor earnings for the quarter.

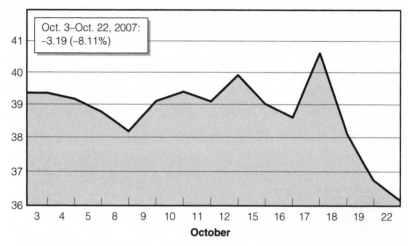

Figure 14.1 eBay stock, October 2007

The previous quarter the Earnings Runner trend was visible once again. In the second quarter of the year, eBay announced earnings on July 18.

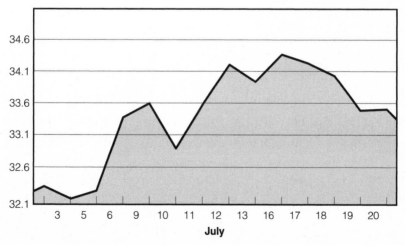

Figure 14.2 eBay stock, July 2007

Between July 3 and July 16, the stock did very well. The previous quarter the trend occurred once again.

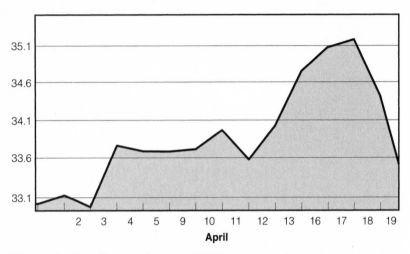

Figure 14.3 eBay stock, April 2007

I encourage you to go to Google Finance or Yahoo! Finance and see how reliable the Earnings Runner trend has been for eBay in the last few years. Also look at the hot stocks like First Solar and Apple. You'll undoubtedly notice that the trend doesn't occur every

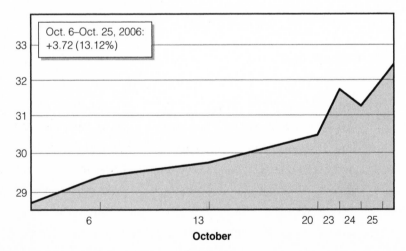

Figure 14.4 eBay stock, October 2006

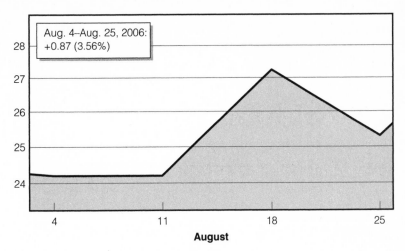

Figure 14.5   eBay stock, August 2006

quarter. No trend is 100 percent reliable. But it occurs most of the time. Take a look at a couple of more occurrences of the Earnings Runner trend with eBay going back a little while. The first shows the time leading up to the October 2006 earnings report; the second shows the time just prior to the August 2006 earnings report.

Playing the Earnings Runner Trend

How do you make money out of the Earnings Runner trend? The idea is to buy a stock somewhere between five and fourteen days ahead of an earnings announcement. (Sites like Yahoo! Finance can give you the dates of earnings announcements. My company's Web site has this info as well—http://www.trendfund.com). But you don't want to buy in blindly; you need to have some faith that the trend is likely to occur this quarter. So as earnings report season nears, you need to follow the stock. You're looking for some movement. The stock should appear to start a gradual incline and the volume of trading should be high. (Pretty much every stock chart can combine volume and price into a single chart.) Once you see these indicators, you jump in, buying long positions on the stocks. The hope is that the stock will continue it's upward trend and you'll hold it to just before the earnings announcement. You should sell before the end of the day on which earnings will be released. Or, if the report is expected in the morning, you should make sure you are out of the position by the close of the previous day.

I rarely hold stocks into the announcement of earnings. As far as I'm concerned, that's gambling. You never really know what's going to be announced, and you could get crushed. Just look at the first eBay chart in this chapter for a perfect example of what can happen on a bad earnings report. Furthermore, there are times when a good earnings report will lead to a sell-off. As far as I'm concerned, the best play is to sell just before earnings and avoid the uncertainty as to what the company will report and how the market will react to that report.

· · · · · · · · · · · · · · · · · ·
WAXIE'S TIP

Buy the rumor, sell the news is usually the first stock market trend people are aware of. Buy into earnings (rumor) and sell before the earnings are released (news).

Playing Trends Safely

Any decent trader who makes money over an extended period of time will tell you that nothing in the world of financial markets is a certainty. The most reliable trends fail sometimes. That's why you need to be very careful and not invest too much in any one play—or in any one trend for that matter. Stocks like eBay and Google, which have had very reliable earnings runs in recent years, could really flounder in the days before earnings. Some sort of scandal could roil one of the companies and cause the stock price to cease its earnings run and take a serious dive. Or, on a larger scale, some global political event (perhaps a major terrorist attack) could sour the entire market, sending everything into the tank. One thing that overrules all trends is—*news*. I like to say, "News *rules!*" You can have the best idea ever, but if something newsworthy happens to a stock, or the market, that stock or the market will most certainly react. There's no trend I have ever encountered that will overcome news—if the news is strong enough.

There are two basic ways to protect yourself from the uncertainty inherent in Earnings Runner trades, and both are extremely important. First off, you need to make sure that you're not putting too much money into any one trend play. As you get started with trend trading, *I suggest that you put at risk no more than 1 percent of your trading account in any single trade.* You might even keep that number lower, at about one half of 1 percent, at least until you get comfortable with what you're doing. Even while playing a very small percentage of your portfolio, you shouldn't make more than a couple of Earnings Trend plays at a time because of the risk of a general market downturn.

The second thing you need to manage your risk is to put in stop-loss orders on all Earnings Trend plays. A stop-loss order, for those new to the term, defines a price at which your stock holdings will automatically be sold. Say that you bought stock WAXIE for $25 on an Earnings Run play. You might include a stop-loss order at $23, so that if the stock falls $2 per share you will automatically be traded out of the position, and your loss will be minimized.

Consider your stop-loss carefully before you engage in this or any other trend play (or even if you chose to be an investor). Ask yourself how much are you comfortable losing on the play, then set the stop accordingly. The higher your tolerance of risk, the lower you can put the stop-loss order. And keep your eye on the stock. As it moves into profitable territory you can adjust your stop-loss to follow the rising price of the stock. For example, if you were to buy the stock WAXIE at $25 and the stock moved up to $26.50 in the few days you've had it, you might move your stop loss order to $25.50. You'd lock in some profit that way and be protected against it moving below that.

WAXIE'S SIDEBAR: Thoughts on Stop-Loss Orders

Figuring out where to place your stop-loss order is tricky. You don't want to set the stop-loss too far away from your initial price, or you could lose a substantial amount of money. But you also need to be careful not to set the stop-loss too tight. Think about Google, which at the moment is trading at about $400 per share. With the price this crazy high you're going to expect some movement of a couple of bucks up and down almost every day. A $1 move just isn't all that meaningful for a stock carrying this price. So if you were to buy into Google and set a tight stop-loss order—say .50—you could almost guarantee that you'd get stopped out of your trade without having any opportunity to even see if the trend play worked. For Google I've been using stop-loss orders of about $15 to $20 on Earnings Runner plays. On shorter-term trends (which I'll talk about later), I tend to put the stop-loss on Google in the $3 to $5 range.

When I trend-trade, I make use of what I call the 2 Percent Rule. I don't want to lose more than 2 percent of my trading portfolio on any trend. (You may want to set this threshold even lower.) Using the 2 Percent Rule, if you had a $50,000 portfolio you'd have to set your stop-loss orders so that you couldn't lose more than $1,000 on any single trade. Say I bought 1,000 shares of WAXIE. To adhere to the 2 Percent Rule, I'd have to set my stop-loss order at $1 off the purchase price. Should I buy 2,000 shares of WAXIE, I'd have to set the stop loss at $0.50.

As you can probably see, sticking to the 2 Percent Rule is going to affect the types of plays you can make on certain stocks. For example, say I wanted to play Google on an Earnings Runner trend play, and I was trading with a $50,000 portfolio. To deal with the volatility that comes with the stock, I'd want to allow myself at least a $15 stop-loss. To ensure that I didn't break my 2 Percent Rule I'd have to restrict myself to 80 shares of Google.

I can't say this frequently or emphatically enough: Smart money management is crucial to trend-trading success. Not every trade will work. If you're not being smart about stop-loss orders and putting the 2 Percent Rule in effect, you'll go broke. Things may go well for a while, but being cavalier about risk management will catch up with you.

A Complete Earnings Run Trend Play

One of the stocks that I've liked recently for Earnings Runner trend plays is SunPower Corporation (SPWRA). It's a pretty volatile stock, with lots of movement, which makes it great for trend plays. The following charts show how earnings runs have affected SPWRA.

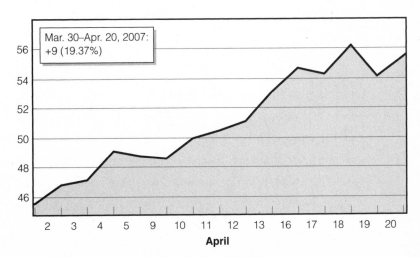

Figure 14.6   SunPower stock, April 2007

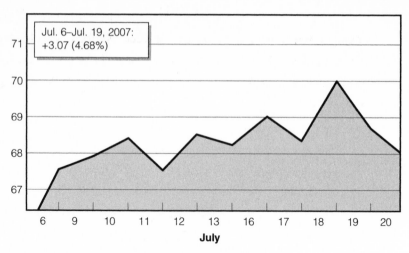

Figure 14.7 SunPower stock, July 2007

So when it came time for the October 2007 earnings report I was prepared to make a trend play. I was on the lookout for some upward momentum in SPWRA starting about ten days before earnings were to be released. I saw some minor movement and decided to buy the stock on October 8, 2007, at a price of $80. As the stock moved up, I played with the stop-loss order, keeping it at about $2 below the actual

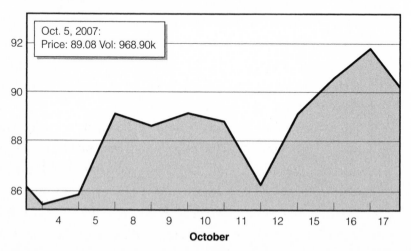

Figure 14.8 SunPower stock, October 2007

price. Then I sold it on October 17, when the stock was at $83.70, netting almost 5 percent in just over a week. Not bad. My clients and I have had some Earnings Runner trend plays that have netted $20 or more in a few days! This is a *very* powerful trend, folks, and it should be respected.

Window Dressing

I think my overall opinion of most highly paid financial superstars has been pretty clear throughout this book, so I don't need to take the time here to mention once again that many fund managers and markets suck. In an earlier chapter, I talked about some of the games mutual fund managers will play to make their funds, and therefore their management, look better than they are. One tactic that unscrupulous mutual fund managers use is so reliable that it has become a trend that I and my trendfund.com clients play almost every quarter.

This trend occurs because every quarter a bunch of mutual fund managers look at their funds' performance and are disappointed. They see that their picks floundered and their return was pretty poor. They know that when new investors start doing research, they will bypass their funds for better performing funds in the same sector. The investors in these funds may sell their shares and look for more capable management. This is bad for fund managers, because the fees they collect are directly determined by the amount they have under management.

So what's a fund manager to do when he realizes he may have to rent out the house in the Hamptons during peak months? He's going to try to make himself look smarter than he actually is. There really aren't too many ways a fund manager can revise history; he can't fake his actual returns or those of his competitors. About all he can do is buy up stocks that performed well during the previous months and sell off those that performed poorly. That way, when it comes time to report on funds' holdings, the manager can say, "Hey look, all winners, no losers. Am I a genius or what?"

I like to say that fund managers are applying *window dressing* to their fund portfolio. And the Window Dressing trend is one you can look to almost every quarter. It's a pretty easy trend to play.

When to Play Window Dressing

This trend shows itself during the last seven to ten days of the financial quarter. During this period, a stock or group of stocks may experience a sharp decline for no apparent reason. These declines can often be attributed to fund managers looking to sell off poor performers over the last few months. The fund managers haven't necessarily lost faith in these stocks. In fact, there's a pretty good chance that the same fund managers will pick up the same stocks once the new quarter begins. So one great Window Dressing play is to look for stocks that take an end-of-quarter dive for no apparent reason. These are potential bouncey-poo stocks once they tank into a quarter's end. You can gobble these stocks up, looking for them to make nice gains once the new quarter begins.

Additionally, when it comes to Window Dressing season, there's a good chance to make some money by playing that quarter's big movers. The stocks that saw the biggest gains could see a bit more upward movement in those final days of the quarter.

Window Dressing Examples

The following chart shows Microsoft's performance in the third quarter of 2006.

As you can see, the quarter was a really good one for the Redmond behemoth. Starting the quarter at just over $22, the stock saw

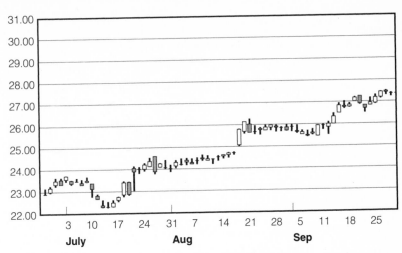

Figure 14.9 Microsoft stock, second half 2006

gains all the way up to the year at close to $27, a gain of about 18 percent. Of course, that's a *huge* leap.

When it came time for mutual fund managers to issue their quarterly reports, they wanted to be able to show their investors that, sure, they had MSFT in their portfolio. You can see by the chart that the recommendation we made to our clients into the quarter's end was very profitable. A lot of ka-chingos to be had for sure!

Here's another Window Dressing play from the third quarter of 2006. Take a look at what happened to THQ Inc. (THQI) that quarter.

The stock did great, starting the quarter at right around $22, then going all the way up to $30. That's a massive jump for a three-month period, and the fund managers wanted to appear as though they saw it coming. We advised our clients to buy on September 21, ten days before the quarter ended, at $29.35. When we saw a little bump in the stock over the next week, we had our clients sell out at $30.66, for a very nice $1.30 gain. Not bad for a week, I think. And these are two *minor* examples. Over the years

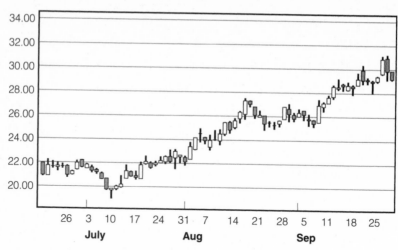

Figure 14.10   THQ Inc. stock, second half 2006

we've had dozens of Window Dressing rockers that have gone for 10 percent, 20 percent, 30 percent, and more, all in a *very, very* short time! Most investors would virtually kill (or die) for returns like that over a year or longer period of time! That, my friends, is the awesome power of Window Dressing! Best of all, it happens in almost every quarter I've tracked it. Doesn't guarantee it will continue, but it should. Fund managers will always want to show how smart they are. You can take advantage of their stupidity!

January Effect

The January Effect is similar to the Window Dressing trend. As a matter of fact, you can think of it as a form of Window Dressing. Fund managers sell off a little more heavily at the end of the year than they do at the close of other financial quarters. They're under a little more pressure to show quality stocks on their books. They often buy back those stocks once the New Year is under way. But a couple of other factors lead to gains in some stocks in January. After the New Year begins, money tends to flow into the market.

When looking for stocks that make sense for a January Effects play, I search for stocks that have sold off through the middle of December but have not yet bounced back. Generally, I'm looking to buy about December 20. And I want to start selling off any January Effect plays by January 5 (more succinctly, by the fifth trading day of January). By then, most of the new money is in the market, and fund managers have reclaimed the stocks they like, so the buying pressure starts to wane.

Here's a January Effect play we made at the start of 2007 for NitroMed, Inc. (NTMD).

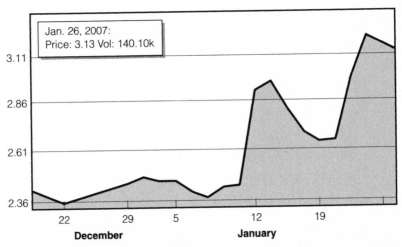

Figure 14.11   NitroMed, Inc. stock, December 2006–January 2007

NTMD had sold off some toward the end of the year, so we advised our clients to buy in just after Christmas at $2.41. We then held until January 12. When the stock hit $2.86, we sold out half, and then sold the other half when the stock hit $2.91.

Here's another January Effect play from 2007. Amgen (AMGN)

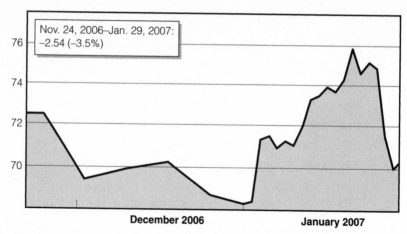

Figure 14.12 Amgen stock, November 2006–January 2007

had had a rough quarter, and had sold off toward the end of the year. We expected Amgen to do nicely in January, so we suggested that our clients buy in at $70 calls in December. We then held the stock until January 11, when we sold out well over $70.

I know it sounds like a cliché, but there are so many January Effects winners over the years it's uncanny. Yes, we've had a few clunkers, to be fair and honest, but the vast majority of these plays have worked very well indeed. January Effects, as have all the trends I've discussed, have made me and countless others a lot of big kachingos!

That's why I say: Trends are your Friends!

Quiz

1. *In what months do financial quarters end?*

   a. March

   b. April

   c. June

   d. September

   e. December

   Answers: a, c, d, e

2. *Using the Earnings Runner, how long before the announcement of earnings should you buy a company's stock?*

   a. 20–40 days

   b. 5–15 days

   c. 2–3 days

   d. 1 day

   Answer: b

3. *Using the Earnings Runner trend, when should you sell the stock?*

   a. Immediately before the earnings announcement

   b. Immediately after the earnings announcement

   Answer: a

4. *When you're getting started, what's the maximum percentage of your account should you risk on any single trade?*

   a. 1 percent

   b. 2 percent

   c. 5 percent

   d. 10 percent

   Answer: a

5. *The tool that automatically trades you out of position when the stock slides to a certain price is known as what?*

   a. Auto trade

   b. Auto sell

    c. Stop-loss order

    d. Fail-safe order

Answer: c

6. **When mutual fund managers sell off losing stocks and buy winners at the close of a quarter, they create what trend?**

    a. January Effect

    b. Earnings Runner

    c. Window Dressing

    d. Gap Ups

Answer: b

Chapter 15

Trading the Gaps

One of my favorite trading plays—the one I make more than any other—is called *trading the gaps* and it's great for people who are busy most of the day and don't have a lot of time to devote to following a bunch of stocks for many hours at a time. Most of the work involved with gap trading occurs in the first hour after the market opens. So even someone who's retired could devote a couple of mornings a week to playing the gaps and making some income off this very common and reliable trend, and that someone could be you! You can trade gaps every day, a few mornings a week, or whatever suits your schedule. Okay, so you're now officially saying to yourself that this seems nutty, right? Wrong! Read on. Trust me, it's well worth your while.

So what's a gap? A gap occurs when the price of a stock opens higher or lower than the closing price of the previous day. Just take a look at the following chart for JA Solar Holdings (JASO) and you'll see clear gaps in the price from one day's close to the next day's open. On October 18, the opening price was slightly lower than the previous day's close; on October 22, the opening price was quite a bit lower than the previous day's close, and on October 23, the open price was a little higher than the previous day's close.

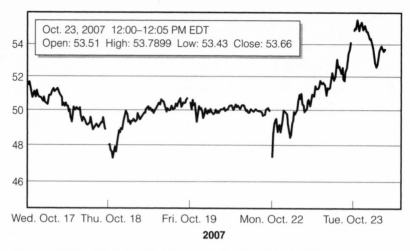

Oct. 23, 2007 12:00–12:05 PM EDT
Open: 53.51 High: 53.7899 Low: 53.43 Close: 53.66

Wed. Oct. 17   Thu. Oct. 18   Fri. Oct. 19   Mon. Oct. 22   Tue. Oct. 23
2007

Figure 15.1   JA Solar Holdings stock, October 2007

These gaps came about because trading does not end at the close of a business day. Most trading occurs between 9:30 A.M. and 4:00 P.M. This is when the big trading floors are in full motion, with bunches of traders for investment houses screaming into phones and monitoring banks of computer monitors. At 4:00 P.M. most of this trading comes to a close, but there's still some after-hours trading.

With relatively few people trading stocks then, there's a tendency for stock price moves to be more extreme then they'd be during the day. When there's some pressure on the stock on either the upside or the downside, there aren't the masses out there to act as a moderating force. So before the market opens, prices have a tendency to jump or dive a little more than they often should. Hence the gap!

There are two types of gaps, Gap Ups and Gap Downs. A Gap Down occurs when the market as a whole or a particular stock opens *lower* than its close the day before. So, for example, if the Nasdaq National Market closes today at 2920 and tomorrow it opens at 2912, then you would say that the Nasdaq *gapped down* 8 points (2920 − 2912 = 8 points). If it closes today at the same 2920 and tomorrow it opens at 2942, then it *gapped up* 22 points (2942 − 2920 = 22 points). Notice that in the previous chart for JA Solar Holdings there are two Gap Downs and one Gap Up.

Many times the market gaps up or down for no apparent reason; there's no news events or anything else that would seem to cause the change in price. But sometimes there's after-hours news that causes the gap. For example, if Google (GOOG) reports stellar earnings today and totally blows past expectations, then chances are that the tech sector as a whole is going to Gap Up. This makes a certain sense, right? GOOG carries a lot of weight and has a large market cap; its earnings have (at least at the time of this writing and since it came public a couple of years ago) what we call "market mover status."

The play, the way to make money, is to *fade the gap,* which means we make a purchase assuming that the gap is going to close soon after trading starts and volume comes into the market. That means that if a stock gaps up, we want to sell it short. If the market opens lower (gaps down), we like to buy it with a long position. We *fade* it either way!

For many people out there, this technique is totally counterintuitive. If a stock has fallen overnight, there's a gut reaction that your best play is ride the momentum down and follow the bearish trend. But you need to fight this natural tendency.

It will help if you think of a gap as you would a rubber band. A market gaps up or down based on pre-market buying and selling on light volume. The stock moves are vastly overdone and exaggerated, which creates pressure. It's like pulling at the ends of a rubber band. And what happens when you stretch a rubber band and then let it go? It will always *snap back* (ever hear the term "snap back rally"; it comes from this), and the cool thing is, it not only will snap back, but if the rubber band is pulled far enough apart it'll snap back well beyond the starting point! Try it if you don't believe me!

For those looking to save for retirement, Gap Downs are a better play than Gap Ups for a couple of reasons. The primary reason is that you're not going to be able to play a Gap Up in your IRA. To properly fade the Gap Up, you'd have to short-sell the stock, which isn't permitted in IRAs. But even if you're trading out of a broker-age account, you may want to stick with Gap Downs, at least for a while. This is because Gap Downs are a little more reliable. Gener-ally speaking, there's an upside bias in the market. People are hope-ful, and they're looking for a reason to buy. And when a lot of folks see a Gap Down, there's a good chance that a lot of them are going to see a potential bargain, which will lead them to buy up the stock.

Playing a Gap Down

Here's an example of how I recently played a Gap Down. This was in the middle of October 2007. I was watching one of the stocks I like to keep a close eye on: First Solar, Inc. (FSLR).

On this day FSLR closed at $134.95, and it opened the following day at $132.76, just over $2.00 lower. No doubt about it, that's a Gap Down.

I usually like to buy this type of stock at the opening of the mar-ket, right at 9:30 A.M. In this case, I bought FSLR at $132.76 and placed an appropriate stop-loss (a price at which I have to bail and take my loss and move on). This stop-loss was at $2.00. As I dis-cussed in the previous chapter, you can't have the stop-loss too nar-row or too large. If it's too narrow, you can't deal with the inevitable minute-to-minute swings; if it's too large, you risk losing more than you'd like. So a $2.00 stop-loss on a stock of $135 is just about right.

....
WAXIE'S TIPS

The higher the stock price, the larger the stop-loss generally is. So, GOOG at $550 would have a roughly $5 stop-loss on a short-term trade and ERTS at $50 would have a stop-loss of roughly $1 on a short-term trade.

....

For longer-term investing I still recommend having a stop of roughly 10 percent. If your stock keeps dropping, something is usually wrong, and holding a perpetual loser not only costs you your principal, but also ties up your capital so you can't earn anything on it on a potential winning investment.

Once my position and stop-loss were in place, I watched the stock until 10:00 A.M. Then, assuming I didn't get stopped out of the trade, I looked at what the low and the high of the day were to that point. These are crucial numbers, and we'll return to them shortly. For the day I placed this trade the low prior to 10:00 A.M. was $131.80 (so I didn't get stopped out).

This is a trend play, not an investment, so I'm not going to hold this stock indefinitely. With this sort of trade, I'm looking to get at least $1.50 reward on every dollar I risk. My stop-loss is at $2 per share, so that means that to get the profit I'm looking for, I'd have to sell when the stock gains $3 on the day. If the stock makes that $3 gain, I'll sell half my shares right there. Sometimes the market doesn't give me that $3, so I adjust accordingly, but that comes with practice. But in this case, it worked like a charm, and FSLR went to as high as $136.20 in the first hour.

I took a $3 profit on half the shares I owned, then, a little later, when the price began to slide a little, I sold the other half at $135.76.

A *very* nice trade indeed!

Think about it: Most investors would kill for 2 percent growth in a month (or two months), and yet here we were, making over 2 percent in less than an hour on our money!

Did someone say, *ka-chingo!* Yeah, it was *meeeee—Waxieeeee!*

Now, let's look at FSLR a little closer. The stock did make that pretty little $3+ move in the first hour for us, but then it pulled back dramatically. I still want to have my $2 stop-loss in as the stock price moves my way. We call this strategy a *trailing stop,* meaning that when FSLR hit a high of $136.20, we would move our stop at $134.20 on the last remaining shares. That's still a very nice profit for us on the second half of the shares I traded. And as you can see by the chart, the play was correct, because the stock then went all the way down to near its low of the day again.

Remember, I had you mark the high and low as of 10:00 A.M. We use these prices to enforce what I call the "Ten A.M. Rule." With the Ten A.M. Rule, you would bracket the high and the low of the day as of 10:00 A.M.

The first part of the Ten A.M. Rule regards stop-losses. If you are still long in FSLR anytime after 10:00 A.M., then your stop is the *lesser* of the two rules:

Waxie's Stop Rule 1: You still have your original trailing stop in place, in this case $2.

Waxie's Stop Rule 2: The low of day (LOD) as of 10:00 A.M. now becomes your stop-loss if it's a tighter stop than the trailing stop you already had in place. With FSLR if you still owned it after 10:00 A.M., and it never made the nice upside move it eventually did, then the LOD as of 10:00 A.M. was $131.80, which was less than $1 lower than your entry price. So, now your risk/reward is that much greater. The most you can lose is about 96 cents, and you're still looking for that same $3 or more move to the upside. That's a *tremendous* risk/reward ratio.

With the Ten A.M. Rule, you also bracket the high of the day (HOD) and if the stock breaks the 10:00 A.M. high, then you can either rebuy FSLR, or you can take the trade again, for the first time. These breaks higher or lower than the Ten A.M. Rule often happen later in the day and they can be important and profitable entries to watch for profitable trades.

The really, really cool thing about this is this type of trade happens nearly *every single day!*

Further Information

Trading gaps is one of the more straightforward trend trades. But before you take on gap trading for yourself, I'd recommend that you spend some time looking at how gaps play out in the real world. Pick a few stocks that you like to follow and track them for a few days. Do they open higher or lower? How do they then react after gapping up, or gapping down? Some stocks react more consistently than others. Once again, I've found that the best way to play most trends is to follow the hot stocks. If solar stocks are hot, then try FSLR and SPWRA (or whatever currently is the stock du jour (there are always a few!) and see how they react each day off the opening price.

. . . .
WAXIE'S TIP

Hot stocks that Gap Down are very high percentage plays in anything but the worst bear market. Investors are optimistic by nature, so the market usually has a positive bias. I tell my clients all the time that people would rather lose in a bear market than miss a big rally. *No one* **wants to miss a "bottom."**

If you need more information on playing gaps, we have several great DVDs at the trendfund.com online store that go more in depth into this winning strategy. And it's not just me who says it's a winner. *Kiplinger's* tried our system without our knowledge, and their caption (and whole article) can be found on our Web site. The writer said, "It works!" You will say the same thing, too!

Quiz

1. *If a stock has gapped down overnight, what would be the right gap play?*
   a. Take a long position (assuming the stock will recover)
   b. Take a short position (assuming the downward momentum will continue)

   Answer: a

2. **What generally causes a gap to close in the early hours of trading?**

   a. Additional volume that stops the extremes of the overnight low-volume market

   b. News on a stock or sector

   c. General daily fluctuation

   d. Seasonal trends

   Answer: a

3. **Which is the better gap play for those getting started in trend trading?**

   a. Gap Ups

   b. Gap Downs

   Answer: b

4. **On a gap play of a $100 stock, what's an appropriate stop-loss order?**

   a. $1

   b. $2

   c. $10

   d. $20

   Answer: c

5. **In addition to your trailing stop-loss order on all gap plays, an additional stop-loss should be placed on the high and low of stocks trading by what time of day?**

   a. 10:00 A.M.

   b. 11:00 A.M.

   c. 1:00 P.M.

   d. 4:00 P.M.

   Answer: a

Chapter 16

Trading Options for Retirement

Want to see your typical financial planner hit the ceiling? Tell him you've discovered that trading stock and index *options* is a great way for you to help prepare for retirement. He'll go ballistic, telling you that you're nuts. Trading options, he'll say, is gambling. You might as well go to Vegas and put your money on black. You'll probably need to give him a Xanax to get him back in his chair. Good, give it to him, and then go make your money on your own! He'll listen to you as soon as he realizes it's *your* way or the highway, and when he sees the mega returns you may just start generating! And that's exactly what it should be. Remember, this is about *your* retirement, not about your helping your advisor in *his* retirement!

On this topic, as with so many others, the financial analysts are wrong—*dead* wrong. Options, if used correctly, can add a strong element of safety and stability to your IRA or other retirement account, in my experience and my not-so-humble opinion.

Moreover, you don't have to be a market wiz to get involved with options. At the basic level this stuff is really pretty easy, and you can make some money with minimal risk, as you'll see in the following pages. My clients at trendfund.com are often initially intimidated by options because of what they have heard about them from people who aren't truly familiar with them. Usually, once clients see how darn easy trading options can be, they can't wait to start using them to enhance their own trading and their retirement. As with anything else, though, if this isn't appealing to you, that's totally cool, dudes and dudesses. In life we take what we need and leave the rest behind if we want to be successful in any endeavor. What works for me may or may not work for you. Having said that, let's see if we can get you excited enough to try options!

You will need to learn a few concepts and some vocabulary. Dealing with the vocabulary may be the hardest part of the whole process. Once we get through the underlying concepts and the language we use to talk about options, we'll look at some techniques that I believe will help you add to your portfolio's ka-chingo value.

What's an Option?

First and foremost, you need to understand what an option is. To help get your head around it, imagine that the following extremely unlikely scenario happens to you. (Note: I'm writing this chapter toward the end of summer, when the produce at New York's farmers' markets has been excellent.)

You're at a local market, where you happen to see Martha Stewart, Rachel Ray, and Mario Batali standing in front of a fruit vendor. They're extolling the virtues of cantaloupe. They all agree that the melon is delicious and largely ignored by most cooks. Rachel says something about planning an all-melon week on her show; Mario muses that he might make March melon month; and Martha says that her next magazine will be devoted entirely to the virtues of that beautiful orange flesh.

By sheer coincidence, that very night, you happen to stumble across the Weather Channel, where you hear about a drought devastating the melon-producing regions of Chile.

You hear all this and think to yourself, *Man, this would be a great time to own a lot of melons. The prices could very well skyrocket!*

You go home and do some research and see that you can buy cantaloupe for $1 per pound.

But as you think about buying in, you come to realize that you
have two potential problems:

1. You have a limited amount to invest. You only have $1,000 to put into
this venture. That doesn't seem like nearly enough to invest in this
great opportunity.

2. You're a little scared. TV chefs are known to be flaky, and weather
people are consistently wrong. What if the new recipes never appear
and Chile has a bumper crop. Do you really want to risk a big portion
of your savings?

You think about the dilemma for a while, then you come up with
a very clever solution. You head to California, where you talk to the
world's largest supplier of cantaloupe. Both you and the supplier
know that cantaloupe is now selling for $1 per pound on the open
market. You say to him that you'd like the right, but not the obligation, to buy every pound of cantaloupe in his field for $1.25 per
pound anytime within the next month.

In return for that right, you're willing to pay him, right now, in
cash, 10 cents for every pound of cantaloupe in his field.

The two of you talk over the potential deal. It seems there are upside and downside risks for each of you.

Upside for the Supplier

- *Cash today.* There's no guarantee he'll get any more than the current market rate, so the extra 10 cents per pound seems like found
money.

- *Possible continued ownership of his asset.* The supplier knows that
you are not going to buy his crop if the price doesn't get above
$1.25 per pound. Why would any buyer purchase something he'll

have to sell at a loss? So he may be able to pocket the 10 cents per pound and keep his cantaloupe.

■ *Protection against a slide in price.* Even if the price of melon drops to 90 cents per pound, he'll still make a dollar per pound, because he's gotten you to cough up that additional 10 cents.

Downside for the Supplier

■ *Limited profit potential.* The most the supplier can make off his crop is $1.35 cents per pound (the $1.25 purchase price plus the 10 cents you paid up front). If the price spikes at $3.50, he'll still have to sell to you at $1.25 and watch as you off-load the same stuff for a huge gain.

Upside for You (The Buyer of the Right to Purchase the Melon)

■ *Limited risk.* The most you can lose is the amount you paid up-front. Let's say Uzbekistan suddenly exports tons of melon, killing the price. You won't have to worry about the nosedive. Whether the melon is at $1.20 or 65 cents doesn't really matter to you. It's all equally worthless to you.

■ *Potential to control a large amount of the asset.* With only $1,000 available, you couldn't buy more than 1,000 pounds of the fruit if you were to shop on the open market. However, using this contract, you have the potential to own ten times that. So if the price spikes, you'll have a ton of potential profit. Imagine the price goes to $3 per pound. If you had bought the cantaloupe outright, you'd have made a nice profit of $2 per pound off the 1,000 pounds you could afford, for a $2,000 profit. With this contract, however, you'd have the right to own 10,000 pounds of cantaloupe ($1,000 of investment at 10 cents per pound). You'd buy it at $1.35 ($1.25 agreed-upon price plus the 10 cents for entering into the contract). Total cost of the 10,000 pounds: $13,500.

You'd then be able to sell the 10,000 pounds for a whopping $30,000. Your total profit: $30,000 − $13,500 = $16,500.

■ *Right to sell the contract.* Let's say that the price of melons doesn't do exactly what you thought. Maybe it goes up only slightly and you'd like to get out of your contract. At any point before the contract expires, you can sell it on the open market, realizing whatever profit or loss accompanies the sale at that point.

Downside for Buyer

■ *Loss of up-front investment.* The contract you made with the supplier stipulates that the contract expires in thirty days. If you don't purchase the melon in that period, your contract expires, the assets return to the seller, and you lose your money.

■ *Limited time for result.* Your predictions may come true. The publicity goes wild and Chile doesn't produce. But if these events don't happen within the time frame of the contract, you're SOL.

That, in a nutshell, is an option. The contract you and the melon supplier entered into has all the elements you'll find in a typical option on the stock market (or any commodity). These include:

■ *The price of the underlying asset (in this case $1/lb. of melon).*
■ *The price at which the option is set ($1.25/lb.).*
■ *The price paid for the option ($0.10/lb.).*
■ *An expiration date.*

Options in the Real World

Now that you have the basic understanding of what options are, we can look at how options are created, bought, and sold on the market— and how you can use them to build and *rule* your retirement accounts.

First off, you're going to need to have an understanding of the language of options. This is where things can seem really confusing. But the concepts really aren't difficult, and once you get familiar with the terms, you'll be talking options like a pro. If you can understand the melon example, you can understand this.

Let's start by looking at a listing for a single option you might see on your broker's online account. Each option gives you the *right,* but not the obligation, to own 100 shares of the underlying stock. So, for each contract, you "own" 100 shares of the underlying stock. The reason why many people are drawn to options is for the leverage it gives even a small portfolio. I have clients who trade options and have turned $5,000 into $50,000 in a pretty short period of time. Buying stocks outright, you would never have that opportunity unless you got extremely lucky.

Let's look at an example to break it down even farther. This one is for Cisco Systems (CSCO).

TABLE 16-1. CSCO (CURRENT STOCK PRICE: $32.05)

STRIKE PRICE	BID	ASK	LAST	VOLUME
$32.5	$1.00	$1.10	$1.05	3,690

This listing is for a *call option*. A call is, simply, the right to buy, but again, not the obligation, 100 shares for each contract at a specific price. If you were to buy the option listed here, you'd have the right to buy 100 shares of CSCO at 32.5 any time before the option contract expires. In this example, $32.5 is known as the *strike price.*

How much will the option cost? The current asking price is $1.10 per contract. In the world of options, the price you pay for the option is known as the *premium.* I like to look at it a bit differently, but it's the same net result. I use the following formula: The strike price *minus* the stock's actual price *plus* the option contract price is the *true premium.*

So, let's use the above as an example. The strike price is $32.50. Cisco's stock price is actually $32.05, a difference of $0.45 cents ($32.50 − $32.05 = $0.45). Now we add in the $1.10 price of the call option contract ($1.10 + $0.45 = $1.55) and we have our true premium, which is $1.55. This means that if we were to hold the option until it expires, then CSCO would have to go up *more* than $1.55 for us to profit from this trade. Now, one caveat is, if CSCO (the stock) were to go up *before* the option expires, let's say two days after you bought this call we are referring to, then you should make money even if Cisco only moves 10 cents or 20 cents or for sure 50 cents. Why? Because the premium or true premium you are paying is based on basically *three* things: first, *time* value; second, *price* (leverage); third, *volatility*. (More on these factors to come.)

Cisco is a relatively "steady" stock. Its price most of the time moves up or down with the overall market, and the moves are consistent with the moves of the market in general, or at least have been. In other words, if the S&P or the Nasdaq were to move 5 percent in a year, Cisco in theory would be up roughly 5 percent on the year. Of course, it's not an exact science, and Cisco could and has under- or outperformed the indexes at times.

Before we move on, let's look at the math of this particular option. How can you make money off the purchase of this call option?

At the moment, the option is worthless. While the strike price is greater than the stock price, you wouldn't want to exercise the option. There'd be no point in buying the stock at $32.50 for the sake of selling it at $32.05. In the option world, we say that the stock has no *intrinsic value*. Or you might say that the options are *out of the money*.

It's important to note here that even if the option climbs *into the money* (the point where the stock price is greater than the strike price), you can still book a loss on the transaction. In order for you to actually profit on this option, Cisco is going to have to do some serious climbing.

You'd need to sell the shares for more than the sum of the strike price and the premium ($32.50 + $1.10 = $33.60) to see any profit.

Okay, so let's look at a stock like Google (or Googleicious as I refer to it). The premiums on the options are Google-crazy! Why? Because Google can go up or down 5 percent in a single day, and often
does. Plus, the stock price has been anywhere from the $200s to the
$700s, as I write this, over the last two years or so. Even if Google
wasn't so volatile, the option market makers are still going to charge
you a premium to own a high-priced stock for so little.

STRIKE	LAST	CHANGE	BID	ASK	VOLUME	OPEN INTEREST
610	94.20	−4	92.20	92.90	6	515
620	92.80	0	84.80	85.40	0	2,307
630	77.70	−1.30	77.60	78.30	6	3,620
640	74.70	+1.20	70.90	71.40	7	1,744
650	65.70	−1	64.30	64.90	50	1,828
660	60.30	−0.65	58.10	58.70	15	1,416
670	53.38	−0.62	52.20	52.80	8	1,443
680	48.50	+0.10	46.70	47.30	68	2,866
690	41.70	−4.40	41.60	42.10	39	1,233
700	37	−4	36.70	37.40	148	5,633
710	32.62	−2.36	32.40	32.90	94	2,296
720	29.50	−0.70	28.40	28.80	103	2,680
730	24.50	−2.30	24.60	25.10	26	2,798
740	21.80	−3.20	21.30	21.80	4	1,034
750	19.30	−0.80	18.30	18.80	221	2,780

WAXIE'S SIDEBAR: Intrinsic Versus Extrinsic Value

Often, a buyer will purchase an option that is out of the money. The
strike price of the call option is higher than the stock price, so the option, at the moment of sale, is worthless. Knowing this, why would the
buyer purchase the option? Because there's still time before the op-

tion's expiration. He's buying the time and hoping that something useful happens for him before the option expires. He's buying a $31.95 stock for $2.10 (or actually for $2.65 since the $32.50 strike price is 55 cents more than the $31.95 stock price) thinking or hoping that it'll be higher than $34.60 by the time the option expires. If Cisco were to go to, let's say, $40.60 during that time frame, then the $32.50 call option would be worth $8.10 and he'd nearly triple his investment. He paid $2.10 and he can collect $8.10. That, my friends, is a *big ka-chingo*, and that, my friends, is the potential options give you. And, yes, my clients at trendfund.com and I have had so many 100, 200, and even 1,000 percent "winners" that your head would spin around if you had done it yourself.

In the options world, this time value is known as *extrinsic value*. There is an actual standard calculation to determine the extrinsic value of an option. As stated above, the equation considers the time remaining, the price of the stock, the stock's historic volatility, and other factors.

A Swiss Army Knife of the Market

Options are extremely flexible and powerful. They can be used to make the most of market trends, either up or down. Or they can be used to hedge a position. You can get as sophisticated and complex with options as you want. You can read and study for a very long time in order to learn how to get the most out of options. But for this book, and for the sake of your retirement account, we're going to limit the scope of our options discussion. You'll learn all the basics, as well as the way options can work for you in retirement.

Use of Options in Retirement

There's a limited amount of options trading that is allowed by law in retirement accounts. There are a number of sophisticated and risky plays you can make with options that aren't available in most IRAs or Keoghs. There are federal laws preventing some of these transactions, and brokerage regulations, too. Pretty much every brokerage on the planet requires you to submit some paperwork before they will allow you to trade options. They're trying to protect themselves from lawsuits by making their clients jump through hoops while screaming, "Yes, I know the risks."

A lot of the fancier options stuff I'm not going to bother covering here. There are two reasons. The first is that you won't be able to make these sorts of trades in your retirement account even if you want to. Secondly, even if you could execute some of these techniques, you probably shouldn't. It requires a lot of study and management to make some of the more esoteric plays work. There can be a lot of risk. As the saying goes: No potential pain, no gigantic gain! Or something like that.

When it comes to options trading for retirement, we're going to focus on one technique called the *covered call*. This is something I think that just about everyone should be doing in their IRAs. After you hear an explanation as to what a covered call is, I think you'll be calling your broker to set up options trading in your account. Yes, it can be *that* powerful a technique.

After the discussion of covered calls, I'll talk about some of the other ways in which people use options. With these, I'll just cover the concepts briefly. If you want to pursue them further, I'd recommend some serious study. The Options DVDs package from trendfund .com will get you started on the right foot.

The Covered Call

There are certain stocks that a great number of people have in their retirement accounts. These include superlarge tech companies as well as traditional blue-chip stocks. If you're like most, you have some shares of Microsoft, Cisco, Exxon, General Electric, and maybe even new blue chips like Google or Apple Computer and you've likely been told by your financial analyst or by another book that you're simply holding these stocks because they offer great long-term value. That is, you'll hold them, and as the companies grow, their stock price will rise and they'll appreciate in value. Or they will simply throw off a dividend, so even if the stock price doesn't appreciate, the dividend allows you to build your retirement savings. That's assuming the stock doesn't go *down* more than your dividend covers. Then you are plum out of luck.

I've got my concerns about these stocks, but I'm not going to try to convince you to offload them. If you're comfortable with them, by all means keep them. But while you're holding these stocks, you can use options to generate a little, and sometimes more than a little, income from your holdings.

Here are the basics of the covered call. Say you have 500 shares of Cisco in your IRA. You go to your online broker and look at the options market for Cisco. On the day I wrote this chapter, these are some of the options that were available. At the time, Cisco's stock was trading at $30.80.

CALLS	LAST SALE	NET	BID	ASK	VOL	OPEN INT
07 Sep 27.50 (CYQ IY-E)	3.50	−0.10	3.70	3.80	13	5358
07 Sep 30.00 (CYQ IF-E)	1.35	−0.25	1.35	1.45	997	36266
07 Sep 32.50 (CYQ IT-E)	0.25	−0.05	0.20	0.25	697	39457
07 Sep 35.00 (CYQ IG-E)	0.05	0.0	0.0	0.05	30	13705
07 Oct 27.50 (CYQ JY-E)	3.70	−0.30	3.80	3.90	19	40926
07 Oct 30.00 (CYQ JF-E)	1.80	−0.25	1.85	1.95	129	63880
07 Oct 32.50 (CYQ JT-E)	0.65	−0.15	0.60	0.70	91	34022
07 Oct 35.00 (CYQ JG-E)	0.15	−0.05	0.15	0.20	56	16626

244 Rule Your Freakin' Retirement

This table is a little more involved than the last, but most of the information should be familiar to you now. Take a look at the first entry.

The first information you have is the date the option expires (07 Sep—September 2007). All stock options expire on the third Friday of the listed month.

Then you have the strike price, which for the first row is $27.50. You should immediately notice that the option price is lower than the stock price of $30.80, so you'd say that this option is *in the money*. That is, the holder of this option would be better off buying the stock at the agreed upon price and selling it, rather than letting the option expire. Still, that person would not immediately profit by buying the option, claiming the stock, then turning around and selling it on the open market. His or her total cost for a share would be $31.30 (the $27.50 strike price plus the $3.80 per option contract equals $31.30). That means he or she is paying a true premium of 50 cents ($31.30 − $30.80 = $0.50).

If you wanted to, you could initiate your own option just like this one. You'd *sell* the option for $3.70 per share and sell the actual stock for $27.50, which would net you $31.20 per share, which is just a little bit higher, 40 cents, than the actual stock price. So you'd make a small profit by selling this option if the price remained flat through the expiration date. You wouldn't make much, but it is something.

Now take a look at the second-to-last row in the table. This is an October call, and will expire the third Friday in October. Here the strike price is out of the money—the strike price is higher than the stock price. The buyer of this option would have to wait for the stock to rise $2 above its current price before it had any value. The cost of the option is 60 cents per share.

This particular option offers you an interesting opportunity for profit. To understand how, let's run through some possible scenarios.

WAXIE'S SIDEBAR: Information in the Options Table

In the options table (see page 239) the last two columns give key information. The column labeled "Vol" shows how many options are changing hands in a given time period. A low number shows that there's little interest, while a high number shows the opposite.

The open interest column shows the number of option contracts that have been created at that strike price and expiration date. A high number in the open interest column shows that it's a popular item.

Scenario 1. Cisco Stays Where It Is

One possibility is that Cisco stays flat. It neither rises nor falls a whole lot in the period prior to the expiration. That's quite likely, because for the last few months, Cisco hasn't moved much one way or the other. The following chart shows how even-keeled it has been.

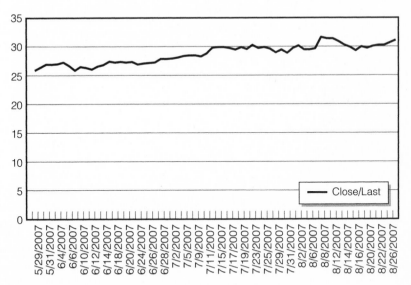

Figure 16.1   Cisco stock, May–August 2007

If this flat trend remains, and Cisco stays in the neighborhood of $31, you'll do quite well on this option. The option will expire worthless; you won't have to sell your shares. You get to keep the 60 cents per share premium you collected for entering into the option contract. Before you say "Big deal, making sixty cents on a stock is *nothing!*" consider this: While 60 cents per share doesn't seem like a lot, it's nearly 2 percent in a month! Compounded annually it would net you over 20 percent potentially! Snicker at that, dude. I dare ya!

Scenario 2. Cisco Stock Increases

Imagine that Cisco has a substantial increase in its stock price. Given the stock's recent history, 10 to 12 percent in a short time would be lot. For the sake of this example, however, imagine that the stock increases 15 percent in a short time, to where it's trading at $34.30.

You don't make out so bad here either. For starters, you sell the stock for $32.50 per share and you collect the 60-cent premium ($32.50 strike price, plus $0.60 the price of the call option = $33.10).

The downside here is that you miss out on some of the profit. In total you collect $33.10 per share, whereas if you had held the stock, you'd have all the profit that came with the rise in price. Of course, if Cisco went through the ceiling, you'd be kicking yourself for not just holding the stock and getting the value out of it that way. But Cisco hasn't gone through the ceiling in a very long time. As with anything else, you are playing the proverbial percentages.

Scenario 3. Cisco Stock Price Falls

Say that Cisco drops in value. It goes from about 31 down to 25. This isn't terrific for you because at the end of the option period you'll still own the stock. Having sold a covered call on the option doesn't protect you from all of the downside that comes with a fall in the stock price.

However, having sold the covered call does make things a little better for you. You've gotten some value out of having collected on the premium. In fact, by having sold the covered call, you've given your-

self some downside protection. If the stock drops a small amount—
less than 60 cents—you still come out ahead.

WAXIE'S SIDEBAR: Calls and Puts

There are two broad categories of options: calls and puts. For the sake
of your retirement accounts you'll be sticking to calls. But as you're learning about this topic, you should understand what puts are.

As we've discussed, when you buy a call option, you're purchasing the
right to buy 100 shares of a stock at a specific price. A put is exactly the
opposite: You're buying the right to sell a stock at a specific price. You'd
buy a put option when you believe a stock is going to decline in value.

Say that you believe that the stock WAXIE, which is trading at $33
per share is going to plummet to $20. You'd do well to buy a put option,
reserving the right to sell the stock at $30. When the stock hits $20,
you'd sell it at $30 and pocket the difference ($10).

A put is the option equivalent of selling short. It's a way to make money
when the market falls.

Note that put options are just like call options, in that they both have
strike prices, premiums, and are said to be in and out of the money at
different times.

Choosing a Stock for a Covered Call

You shouldn't run out and buy a stock for the sake of making money
off it with a covered call. Rather, you want to use covered calls on
stocks that you own and want to keep in your portfolio—stocks that
you've decided you want to own in the long term. When you believe
a stock's a dog—that it's not going anywhere—you should just sell it
and get your money in something that you believe in. When you believe that a stock is going to go through the roof, you might buy it
outright, or buy some call options yourself.

As I already mentioned, many people have a deep belief in the long-term benefit of owning a stock like Cisco. These people would do well to consider using covered calls.

The stocks in your portfolio that will do well with a covered call are those that, like Cisco, have been pretty stable. They've had some small, steady gains in the past year or so, but they haven't set the world on fire recently, and there's no good reason to believe that they will in the immediate future. When the stock stays stable, you'll make your money on the option's premium, while holding on to the stock. You gain some income while you wait for the stock's long-term prospects to rise.

Some stocks you might want to consider include: General Electric (GE), Microsoft (MSFT), and IBM. There are others, but you should get my drift. You want stocks that are slow and steady. With Google or Amazon you could hit a home run, but you could also get hammered. Having said that, if you are a real risk taker and you own some of these stocks in your IRA, then by all means look into using covered calls to capitalize on the *huge* premiums you could capture each month. Having said that, usually if you pick the right stocks, as in the Cisco example, you could capture 2 to 3 percent *per month* on many stocks without breaking a sweat. I've known investors who have netted 25 to 40 percent per year using this very same technique—year after year!

WAXIE'S SIDEBAR: Covered and Naked

At this point you might be wondering why we use the word "covered" when talking about this method of selling call options. This is because there's an important distinction between two types of options: those that are covered and those that are *naked*.

In this chapter I've been discussing a situation where you sell options on stock that you actually own. I've been using the example of Cisco, because I feel sure that many of the readers of this book will have that stock in their IRAs.

If you sell call options in Cisco and the stock rises beyond the stock price, you could be required to sell off the stock to the buyer of the option. You know that going into the process, and you're aware of the potential losses and gains. If Cisco suddenly does really well, you won't realize all the gain because you'll have to sell the stock at the agreed-upon strike price.

A naked option is far, far riskier. The creator of a naked option doesn't own the underlying stock when he creates the option. Let's say that your crazy friend George is absolutely certain that Cisco (now at $31) will stay flat or lose some value, but he owns no Cisco stock. He could still opt to sell call options where the strike price is a bit higher than the stock price, say $33. He sells the option for a 50-cent premium.

If the stock stays flat, he'll be in good shape. He'll have pocketed the premium and he'll never have to produce the stock because the option is worthless. (Nobody wants to exercise the right to buy a stock at $33 when it's selling on the open market at $31.)

But what if, by some crazy chance, Cisco goes totally bonkers? It goes from $31 to $61 on the day the option expires. Crazy George is screwed. The owner of the option is going to want that stock at the agreed upon $33, and George is going to have to produce it. He's going to have to go to the market, buy the stock at $61 and sell it at $33. Ouch.

There is essentially an unlimited risk when you sell naked options, whereas the gain is limited to the premium you charge. When I lectured at Tulane University's business school (the Freeman Business School) a few years ago, I met a professor there who bragged about how he'd made hundreds of thousands selling naked calls and puts. "Wow!" you say? Well, yes, I do believe he did, but he finished by telling me that he got "caught" because he had sold naked puts on a little company you may have heard of—Enron! When Enron went belly-up, his profits turned to a very large overall loss! He got "caught" *naked!* I prefer to keep my clothes on while in public if you don't mind.

Mechanics of Options

If you want to get involved with options in any way, you need to have a talk with your broker. As I mentioned, options on stock expire the third Friday of the month listed. You need to know how your broker deals with expiring options. If you've bought an option that has value, some brokers will automatically exercise the options, meaning you now own the stock itself. For example if you have ten call options contracts of APPL and they are in the money, you will own 1,000 shares of APPL at options expiration. Some brokers automatically exercise options that have 75 cents or more of value. Any less and you just lose the money—period.

You don't want to miss out on money you deserve just because you fail to make a call to your broker instructing him to sell an option.

When selling covered calls, you won't have a whole lot to do. If things go according to plan, you'll just be collecting the premium, while the option expires worthless. You collect the ka-chingos and rack up what can be rather large percentage gains in your retirement account each and every month!

And if you are confused at all by options, don't sweat it, there are lots of good books on the subject, including *McMillan on Options,* and, of course, we have lots of DVDs and books on the subject of options on my trendfund.com Web site.

All in all, options can be a very powerful means to an end, in this case *retirement.* If you use them responsibly and consistently, you will be well on your way to Ruling Your Freakin' Retirement!

Quiz

1. **For a steady stock that you wish to hold for the long term, which type of option play makes good sense?**

   a. Naked put

   b. Naked call

   c. Covered call

   d. Covered put

   Answer: c

2. **The value of an option that accounts for the time remaining before the option expires is known as:**

   a. Intrinsic value

   b. Extrinsic value

   Answer: b

3. **Creating an options contract without holding the underlying stock is known as:**

   a. A covered option

   b. A free option

   c. A naked option

   d. Insanity

   Answer: c

4. **When do options expire?**

   a. The first Friday of a month

   b. The second Friday of a month

   c. The third Friday of a month

   d. The fourth Friday of a month

   Answer: c

5. **If an option's strike price is $30, and you pay $2.50 for the option, what price will the underlying stock have to reach before you turn a profit?**

   a. $31.00

   b. $27.50

   c. $32.50

   d. $35.50

   Answer: c

Conclusion

Regardless of how you end up managing your retirement, or ruling it, just be clear that you're the one taking the losses and reaping the gains, so be responsible for your own account! There are no victims, only volunteers. The more control you take of your retirement, the more you will, I believe, feel secure and empowered. Too many people far too often have put blind faith into people and institutions that betrayed them, or simply weren't all they were cracked up to be. Either way, all the IRAs that owned Lehman Brothers, Bear Stearns, Washington Mutual, and dozens of others took a serious beating in 2008. Will they recover? Maybe. Maybe not. Will home prices recover anytime soon? Will the economy re-ramp up anytime soon? What will the new administration do? There are many, and I do mean *many* questions that are yet to be answered. That creates volatility and it creates stress for many of us. When it comes to the stock market, if I'm right about the market direction, and I preface this by saying I hope I'm not, then we have a lot further to go down. My downside targets are available and updated at trendfund.com. As I write this, I'm on record with a 4,500 Dow target, and a 700 to 900 Nasdaq target. Those are subject to change. Perhaps they are now much higher, or much lower. The market is all over the place, and that's unlikely to change soon. That makes your retirement, something that should be comfortable and less stressful, very volatile as well. You have to decide if you want to stick with current asset allocation models that include that volatility and risk, or try something different. Either way, suffice to say I think now more than ever *you* need to control *your* retirement!

The difference between taking some control back of your retirement account and sitting idly by watching and praying is very subtle, but potentially life changing!

My strategies are going to be based on my experiences in the stock market and the research I did in writing this book. You may decide to join me in Ruling Your Freakin' Retirement, or you can sit by and watch the money you've worked for your whole life potentially disappear. And, with it, perhaps your chance to retire!

Fools rush in, so don't rush in. It's a marathon, not a sprint to most of the readers of this book. In this day and age it's *extremely* important that *you* think outside the box. Whether you agree with some of the ideas presented here, or you disagree and toss the book in the trash, the idea is to offer different solutions, different possibilities. I'm a firm believer that out of desperation often comes inspiration. I believe if you blindly leave your money in the hands of others, you shouldn't be shocked if you lose some—or all—of it! I wouldn't want to be responsible for anyone else's retirement but my own! That's a helluva lot of responsibility. Assuming you feel the same way, then why would you not take some action on your own and make some choices on your own for *your* retirement?

Hopefully this book gives you enough ideas so that you can make some very powerful changes in your finances relating to your retirement. They aren't for everyone, but they are unique in many respects, and if something appeals to you, you should go for it. If that doesn't work, then try something else. Just make sure you are always using proper money management techniques and that your asset allocation model is something that you have back-tested and you are confident in!

I'd wish you all the best of luck, but I believe that most luck is simply good preparation. Your life, and your retirement is in your hands. Don't let it slip away without a fight.

That's all, folks! Until next time, remember to keep Rulin', cause life's too short to be a patsy!

· · · · · · · · · · · · · · · · · ·
WAXIE'S TIP

Often out of desperation comes inspiration. Life in the twenty-first century has many challenges. Look at these challenges as opportunities and you will hopefully Rule Your Freakin' Retirement and weather them better than most!

Glossary

An excellent source of additional trading-term definitions can be found at http://www.trendfund.com.

401(k) An employer-sponsored retirement plan that is basically a tax shelter. You invest your money (and it can be matched by your employer) before it has been subjected to income taxes.

403(b) A tax-advantaged retirement savings plan available for public education organizations (teachers et al.), some nonprofit employers.

529 Plan Plans can vary from state to state, but a tax-advantaged investment vehicle in the United States designed to encourage saving for the future higher education expenses of a designated beneficiary.

annuity A right to receive amounts of money regularly, and usually in equal installments, over a period of time. Often over the remaining life or lives of one or more beneficiaries.

ARM Adjustable rate mortgage that allows the borrower to change the ARM to a fixed-rate mortgage within a specific time.

ask The price at which a seller will sell a stock. Also known as the offer. The best ask is the lowest quoted price at which a seller will sell a stock at a particular time.

bearish Pessimistic; expecting the market to go down or a stock's price to fall.

bid The price at which a buyer will buy a stock. The best bid is the highest quoted price at which a buyer will buy a stock at a particular time.

bond ladder This is a strategy that was designed to help investors leverage against the risk of interest rate change.

bounce A sudden upward price movement that follows a downtrend and may or may not signal a larger change in direction.

breakout   A new high for the day, or a stock's departure from an established range.

bullish   Optimistic; expecting the market to go up or a stock's price to rise.

buy to cover   To close a short-sale position by purchasing shares to replace the shares borrowed by the account. See *sell short.*

call   An option to buy a stock at a future date at a specific price. See *put.*

cash value policy   The value of an insurance policy if it were to be cashed out before its intended use.

coupon rate   The annual interest rate of a bond.

covered option   A stock call option that you would sell against the underlying security you own.

dead-cat bounce   A bounce that does not signal a change in direction from downtrend to uptrend or rally; instead, a dead-cat bounce is merely a brief interruption in a strong downtrend.

dollar cost averaging   When you buy a stock and it declines in value you buy more at a lower price to average the cost down

estate planning   The overall planning of a person's assets, including the preparation of a will and the planning of taxes after the individual's death.

ETF   Exchange-traded fund that usually tracks a certain sector or country or index in the stock market.

ex-date   The day a stock's share price changes to reflect a stock split and revised number of shares are credited to shareholders' accounts.

extrinsic value   The excess value of an option, over and above the actual underlying equity's price or value

Gap Down   A significant price move down from the previous day's close.

Gap Up   A significant price move up from the previous day's close.

health-care proxy   See *living will.*

(IPO)   Initial public offering is the first time a company sells stock to the public.

intrinsic value   The real value of an equity or stock versus the strike price of an option.

IRA   Individual retirement account is a pension plan with tax advantages that permits individuals to invest through mutual funds, insurance companies, and banks, or directly in stocks and bonds.

ka-chingo!   A nice profit on a good trade.

January Effect   A trend that often occurs at the end of December into the beginning of January whereby stocks that underperformed the market heading into the new year will get bought up by funds, thus driving their prices up abnormally in a short time frame.

Keogh plan   A tax-deferred personal retirement program that can be established by a self-employed individual or small business owner.

living will   A document that defines what an individual wants done in case they are unable to make decisions for themselves before they die. Also called a *health-care proxy* or *power of attorney for health care.*

liquidity   The ability of a stock or other security to be converted into cash quickly and without incurring a loss. The easier the conversion is, the more liquid the stock; if conversion is difficult, the stock is illiquid. Markets often achieve liquidity by having a large number of buyers and sellers.

listed stocks   Stocks that are traded on an exchange, such as the NYSE, as opposed to over the counter.

long-term care insurance   A type of health insurance designed to cover a range of services for people who are chronically or terminally ill.

margin   The capacity to borrow against the securities in your account. Buying on margin means using the shares you hold long as collateral to borrow money to buy more stock.

margin call   A broker's notification to an account holder to sell securities or deposit funds in order to meet a margin requirement. If the account holder takes no action, the broker will liquidate holdings.

maturity date   The final date on which a mortgage or other loan becomes due and payable.

mortgage   A loan that uses real estate as it's collateral.

mutual fund   An open-ended investment company that has a specific investment objective using a diversified portfolio of stocks, bonds, or other securities.

naked option   A call or put option that is sold without the seller holding an underlying security or stock position. See *call, put,* and *option.*

newbie   A new, inexperienced trader.

NYSE Euronext   The New York Stock Exchange, which now owns the European exchange Euronext.

option   A contract giving the owner the right but not the obligation to purchase *(call)* or sell short *(put)* a stock at a particular price by a specified date.

par value   The full face value of a security; i.e., a $5 bill has a par value of $5.

power of attorney for health care   See *living will/health-care proxy*

price chart   The main tool used in technical analysis, in which price movement is charted over time on *x* and *y* axes.

put   An option to sell short a security at a future date at a predetermined price. See *call*.

Roth IRA   An IRA for which contributions are taxed but qualified distributions are not.

secondary mortgage   A second mortgage taken out against the same real estate that was used to secure the first mortgage.

sector   A subset of the market whose component companies are in the same general area of business.

sell short ("short")   To sell a security you do not own in order to make money on a downward price movement.

short squeeze   A sharp stock price move upward, causing short sellers to *buy to cover*.

SIMPLE-IRA   Individual retirement annuities funded with employee elected salary.

SEP   A retirement plan for small businesses that allows employers and employees to contribute to the employee's IRA; subject to special rules on eligibility and contributions.

Social Security   The old-age, survivors, and disability insurance section of the Federal Social Security Act.

spread   The difference between the *bid* and *ask* price of a stock.

straddle   An options play where both a *call* and a *put* are purchased. The call and put have the same strike price, the same expiration month, and the same underlying stock or index.

take long   To buy a stock. See *sell short*.

term life insurance   Life insurance that only provides that insurance for a specified period of time, determined by the individual policy.

trend   A price movement pattern that is represented by different stocks can be relied on to reasonably anticipate the price movement of similar stocks.

trustee   An entity, or person, to whom legal title to property is entrusted to use or manage for another's benefit.

volatility   The degree to which a stock's price moves up and down. A highly volatile stock experiences large price fluctuations, while a more stable stock does not. A particular stock's volatility can vary over time according to market and stock-specific conditions.

Window Dressing   A technique whereby fund managers "dress up" their portfolios to make them look better then they actually are by adding outperforming stocks, and subtracting underperforming ones, at the end of each quarter.

whole life insurance   Permanent life insurance that covers an individual over the course of a life.